Coming of Age
In Scranton

Coming of Age In Scranton

✦

Memories of a *Puer Aeternus*

Terry Carden

iUniverse, Inc.

New York Lincoln Shanghai

Coming of Age In Scranton
Memories of a *Puer Aeternus*

Copyright © 2005 by Terrence S. Carden, Jr.

iUniverse books may be ordered through booksellers or by contacting:

iUniverse
2021 Pine Lake Road, Suite 100
Lincoln, NE 68512
www.iuniverse.com
1-800-Authors (1-800-288-4677)

ISBN-13: 978-0-595-36329-2 (pbk)
ISBN-13: 978-0-595-80765-9 (ebk)
ISBN-10: 0-595-36329-6 (pbk)
ISBN-10: 0-595-80765-8 (ebk)

Printed in the United States of America

To my children, my siblings, their children and their children's children and families in the hope that this will help them understand who we are and where we came from.

Contents

Foreword

I am a Scranton girl. I did not grow up there. I didn't live there for any significant length of time, but I was born there. That makes Scranton my hometown, just as surely as it was my parents'. I was born at **the** Mercy hospital, like my brother before me (yes, the emphasis is on **the**). This is a story of how hometown experiences molded a young man to be what he became, forging a persona that to this day remains somewhat a mystery to me.

My early memories of Scranton center on Prospect Avenue and 17th Street, the childhood homes of my parents, which we visited regularly while my father was in medical school in Philadelphia. I was so young when we left that I have only hazy memories of living there. One Scranton landmark I find it hard to forget is the Coney Island Texas wiener place. It did not have the charm for me that it seemed to have for my father. What's the big deal about an old Greek guy putting chili on hot dogs lined up on his hairy arm? What I remember most is a town that seemed to be dying. I hear it has rebounded somewhat, but I remember the sadness.

My father and I circled each other cautiously throughout my childhood, my adolescence, and as I grew to be a young adult. He didn't get me and yet I yearned for his acceptance. Here the joke was on both of us. I was all of the parts of himself that he could never appreciate until he was much older. I was lucky to understand that by age 35 or so. I also came to appreciate that I resembled my mother enough to drive myself and my father nuts.

But this is not my story, it's my father's. It is a treasure to me. He never shared much of himself, so most of these stories and memories are new ground for me. He explains that he had a compulsion to be in charge. Maybe he really wanted to rule the world. I think he could do it if he had the chance. He is typical of many Scrantonians, willing to work long and hard to achieve whatever goal he sets for himself.

He inspired me to make myself whatever I am and whatever I hope to be. At times he has seemed to be a figure bigger than life—at least to me. These collected memories show that he is much like the rest of us, which is reassuring!

—Andrea Carden Kithianis
Myrtle Beach, S.C.
June 22, 2005

Introduction

When the telephone rang on Sunday morning, April 3, 2005 I was delighted to hear the voice of my niece, Ellen Mrha. She and I had not talked for some time and I was pleased that she had initiated the call. Ellen reminded me that the 15-year anniversary of the death of her mother, my sister Ellen, on April 28, 1990, was fast approaching. She asked me if I talked often with our brother, Edward, and if so, "do you ever talk about mom"? I gave her positive assurances on both counts.

We then talked about her mom and the family for quite awhile, exploring what Ellen told me was some new ground for her. She then asked me if I would try to send her daily recollections of her mother from that day to the date of the anniversary. I agreed that I would try.

That afternoon, I dashed off the first installment, which my wife, Coralie, and I agreed was the most memorable of the recollections we had of the time Ellen lived with us in Illinois just prior to her fatal illness. That installment, reproduced in the epilogue, was produced easily and quickly, but it quickly became apparent that it would be no easy task to follow through daily for 25 days. Additionally, I realized that disjointed images, memories and recollections do not paint a picture of a person. One might remember something, but what did it mean, in what context did it occur.

It also became clear that while I had many memories of the childhood we shared, those memories could only be viewed through the lens of my experience and my recollections of that experience. Presumably, my siblings had many of the same or similar experiences, since we all grew up in the same houses, the same neighborhoods and, for the most part, attended the same schools. They had to experience the same economic and cultural forces, though they may have viewed them slightly differently. I soon resolved to concentrate on reporting my memories, presuming this would suggest how all of us may have been affected by these forces.

As I sat each morning at the computer, composing the day's installment, it occurred to me that recollections of my childhood and young adulthood might prove interesting as well as revealing to my children and others in the family. Then I began to wonder if this was a story worth telling for a wider audience. The first step was limited publication of the 25 installments sent to Ellen by e-mail. The compilation was distributed to a small audience of family members and friends, all of whom were enthusiastic (or was it merely polite?).

That convinced me it would be worthwhile to pursue formal publication of a memoir of that time and place, which I also knew would mean a lot of work. It is one thing to crank out 25 installments of recollections and another to organize those recollections into a coherent body of information for publication. The original totaled some 26,000 words; this version is about twice as long.

While substantially reorganized, virtually the entire original is preserved in this version. The differences are mainly corrections of the original, the addition of factual and historical information to place the recollections in context and the reporting of additional recollections to reflect the scope of the project, which I decided should include experiences through graduation from the University of Scranton.

That in no way implies that I ceased to have interesting experiences when I left Scranton the first time. However, I recognized that the rest of my life had been built on the base constructed during those years, so it made sense to set that as a boundary. In the main, I respected it but at times wandered briefly into the future when that seemed appropriate. Some of the additions represented memories contributed by others. Many of the corrections came from readers of the original. Interested readers can glean the flavor of the original from the two installments reproduced in the epilogue to this version.

I have attempted to produce this in a consistent style, which is mine alone and from which I may have strayed from time to time with no harm done to the reader, I hope. Recollections of their very nature are subject to error, so I worked to confirm those facts subject to confirmation by research. Thank you, Google. I also tried to keep the manuscript relatively free of typographical and other kinds of errors, but know from experience that some always foil even the most meticulous review. Presumably, none will lead the reader astray.

The text is devoid of illustrations or maps, which some readers may consider a deficiency. I attempted to describe events in terms of intersection or street locations when appropriate, presuming that anyone with a genuine interest can easily call up a map of that location on Mapquest at http://www.mapquest.com/main.adp

On a recent trip to Scranton I toured the neighborhood of my childhood and tested some of my personal recollections on former classmates, who pronounced them accurate, in the main. Therefore, I am confident that this work paints a realistic picture of what it was like for at least one person to grow up and come of age in Scranton, PA in the 1940s and '50s. Presumably these experiences were reasonably typical for that place and time.

I should comment here that some readers might be offended by my descriptions of experiences related to the nuns I encountered along the way. Be assured these comments were not meant to be disrespectful or malicious but are merely recollections based on an adult's perspective of what went many years in the past when expectations were different. Since that time I have met and worked with some really terrific—one might even say heroic—nuns who are a credit both to themselves and the church.

When I decided to publish these remembrances I realized that had our parents done this—which was unheard of at the time—their recollections would be treasured today. I have many documents related to my parents, grandparents and even great-grandparents. What I don't have is anything that reflects the day-to-day lives they led, challenges they faced, joys and sorrows they experienced. I can recall reading high school compositions prepared by my father and trying to figure out what he was thinking at the time. If I had had a volume like this to consult, I might have understood him better.

Finally, I am gratified that this has to some extent become a family project. My daughter, Andrea, contributed the foreword, as she did for the original. The cover idea came from my son, Terry, and the cover graphic was created from a photo of our family home on Prospect Avenue taken by my granddaughter, Ann Marie. And then there is the constant support and encouragement from my wife, Coralie, who has suffered though multiple versions as the project moved forward.

Now that it is "in the can," so to speak, I can reflect on the process and admit that I am the greatest beneficiary. Organizing and preserving these memories told me things about myself that had been unappreciated. Had someone asked me a year ago whether I might be interested in such a project, I would have laughed. Wrong again!

Perhaps those who are coming after us will find these vignettes interesting. I hope so.

—Terry Carden
Tucson, Arizona
June 22, 2005

1

Parochial but Proud

In my travels over the years I have encountered few towns that reminded me of my boyhood home, Scranton, PA. Among them are Bisbee and Jerome, AZ. Like Scranton, Bisbee and Jerome are old mining towns with wood frame houses built on the sides of hills. And like Scranton, they have seen better days. Unlike Scranton, they are more primitive in many ways and much more isolated from sophisticated population centers. Yet both are attempting comebacks as artists' colonies.

The story of Scranton, it seems, is an unending saga of attempted comebacks. My memories relate primarily to the years after World War II and the Korean War, when I completed my education there and headed out into the world. For me, the world meant New York City and the Graduate School of Journalism of Columbia University. My experience there profoundly affected the trajectory of my life to this day. But whatever I am or have become rests firmly on the base of the experiences of my life as a child and a young man growing to maturity in Scranton, known at the time as "the anthracite capital of the world."

It was hard for me to appreciate as a child that my hometown had started as an iron and steel center and grew to prominence based on railroad connections to the thriving metropolitan areas of the East and Midwest. I have learned that the Lackawanna Iron & Steel Company had the largest capacity in the nation for the production of iron by the end of the Civil War—pretty impressive. But for me, Scranton's identity was not as a center of iron and steel manufacturing; Pittsburgh claimed that role in the 1940s. Despite its early success, the Lackawanna Iron & Steel Company had moved to Lackawanna, NY, near Buffalo, where it could take advantage of cheap ore transported by Great Lakes freighters from the Mesabi Iron Range of Minnesota. Years later when I visited or passed through Virginia or nearby Eveleth, MN, on my way to Canada for fishing, I felt right at home—just as I feel when passing through Bisbee or Jerome, AZ.

Despite its prominent early steel heritage, the most obvious monuments to Scranton's past were not the massive remnants of abandoned steel furnaces buried in the bluff on the north side of Roaring Brook, just east of the magnificent Lackawanna station. They were not the railroad itself, which was still a major source of transportation and commerce in my early years. They were the depressing residue of several generations of aggressive anthracite mining—an industry that was in serious decline and almost dead just after World War II.

There were abandoned collieries where child laborers had worked 12-and 14-hour days in the breakers, picking slate from the coal as it moved past on conveyors—all for $1 to $3 a week, according to published reports. Older boys actually worked with mature men below the surface, deep in the mines, inhaling dust that would destroy their lungs and risking serious injury or death from tunnel cave-ins. They arose before sunrise and returned home after dark, some of them failing to see the light of day for weeks or months, since days off were few and far between. Researchers who have studied conditions prevalent at the time report that wages were a miserable $12 a week, from which the miners had to pay the company stores owned by the coal barons for the food to feed their families and even for the very picks and shovels needed to perform their work. It's not hard to see why they had trouble covering all their expenses. One mine boss at the time frankly described the plight of these poor souls as "little better than semi-slavery." Eventually, child labor was outlawed, but not before the industrial barons extracted their profits from the misfortune and desperation of the poor.

Given the conditions these unfortunates endured, it is not surprising that early organizers of the United Mine Workers of America were admired by the working people of Scranton, as attested by the statue of John Mitchell on the Courthouse Square. Mitchell was president of the United Mine Workers of America, which struck successfully in 1902 to force the previously untouchable cartel of anthracite mining operators to recognize the union's demands for fair wages and safety measures in the mines. Even President Theodore Roosevelt had to put aside his "big stick" when he recognized the power of the mine union to paralyze the country with winter approaching. He became the first president to intervene in a labor dispute, seeking Mitchell's help in bringing the strike to a close. Mitchell was willing to compromise, but the mine operators remained adamant that they would not deal with the UMWA, resulting in a public relations disaster for their cause. Eventually, the strike was settled, a major victory for organized labor, and Mitchell became a hero throughout the anthracite area.

Other monuments to the mining industry were the culm dumps found throughout the Lackawanna Valley. Culm was a mixture of coal, rock and shale left over after coal was processed at the breaker and sent on to the consumer. It was stored in huge piles that seemed invariably to catch fire, sending fumes of noxious sulfur dioxide through the neighboring communities. Burning culm smells like rotten eggs and, depending on the wind direction, made itself known throughout the valley at various times.

And then there was the famous mine fire in nearby Carbondale. It was said that the mine fire was the largest industry in Carbondale and the biggest threat to what remained of the economy there was that they might succeed in putting it out. In Scranton, there were recurrent cave-ins, with entire homes disappearing into the mines below. Such events were attributed to the "robbing" of pillars as mine operators tried to squeeze the last bit of profit from their holdings. Safety required the miners to leave pillars of coal at certain intervals to support the tunnels. As the coal petered out and miners retreated toward the shafts to the surface, those pillars often were taken out, even though that practice had been made illegal in a hard-fought battle by the labor unions for safety legislation.

Since there had not been active mining within the city limits for years, the subterranean support structure, which had not been maintained, weakened and eventually was unable to support the bedrock above the tunnels. This resulted in a collapse of the earth and rock above into the abyss below, with the cave-in consuming whatever stood on the surface. It was not uncommon for a home to be fully or partially buried in a cave-in. There were apocryphal tales of folks coming to the bottom of their cellar steps only to find that there was no longer a cellar. In Scranton, all basements were known as cellars, and most of them fitted the image. Similarly, it was said that folks long buried at the Cathedral Cemetery were no longer in their crypts, which were reported to have fallen into the mines.

How much truth there was in those tales is hard to say, but there is no question that what were euphemistically called "mine subsidences," known among the populace as cave-ins, were not rare events. The answer: flush silt into the mines at government expense to shore up the surface structures and infuse some desperately needed cash into the economy. Scranton was not too proud to accept a handout from the Federal Government.

Another "industry" for which Scranton became well known along the East Coast in the late 19th and early 20th centuries was prostitution. Scrantonians were proud of many things but that was not one of them. There was speculation that prostitution had been tolerated in a city of God-fearing Christians because it allowed the miners to satisfy their animal urges without threatening the good womenfolk of the town. That may have been partially true, but there is reason to believe that the ladies of the evening provided services to a much wider segment of the male populace. When I left Scranton I encountered no shortage of men who were happy to share with me stories of their deflowering in my hometown. That part of the city's colorful history was not a subject of discussion in polite company. It was generally acknowledged that the prostitution "industry" had been cleaned up at the request of the military prior to the opening an Army base in nearby Tobyhanna either prior to or during World War II. That base, which is now operated by the Signal Corps, continues to be a major employer in North-eastern Pennsylvania.

Employment—or lack thereof—was the prominent issue of day during the entire period of my residence in Scranton. The rest of the nation had recovered from the Great Depression during the war. Scranton had not. Yet Franklin Roosevelt was revered throughout the Lackawanna Valley for what he had done to bring the nation back from the pain of economic ruin. In our home, his likeness shared honor with that of Pius XII, the wartime pope, and the Sacred Heart of Jesus. Another popular icon in the Lackawanna Valley was the infant of Prague, which I am told had to be displayed in a certain manner to achieve divine protection for the home.

Roman Catholic culture was particularly prominent in the Lackawanna Valley, starting with the Irish who were the first primarily Catholic immigrants to arrive, followed by a host of other middle and eastern Europeans. One source reports that "immigrants came to the Anthracite Region from more than three dozen nations, and spoke nearly as many languages. Some were experienced workers; many more were peasants with no industrial job skills." This diversity was reflected in the many neighborhoods and small communities up and down the line extending from Hazleton on the south to Carbondale on the north. Each neighborhood was an ethnic enclave, where folks congregated with "their own."

There were some Catholics among the early settlers in the region, but they were scattered and without priests or churches. The first recorded visit of a priest to the area was that of Father James Pellentz, who traveled from Baltimore up the Susquehanna River as far as Elmira, ministering to the Catholics scattered through this region. The Catholic Encyclopedia reports there were priests among the refugees from the terrors of the French Revolution at Asylum or "Azilum," founded in the 1790s on the banks of the Susquehanna River in what is now Bradford County. It was said that the settlement had been founded as a refuge for the French Queen, Marie Antoinette, who followed her husband to the guillotine before she could flee to America. The settlement was abandoned in 1804 after Napoleon came to power and offered the refugees his protection if they returned.

From that point to the establishment of the Diocese of Scranton, Northeastern Pennsylvania was vassalage of the bishop of Philadelphia, with priests of that diocese being assigned to various communities in the area. Bishop Francis Patrick Kenrick was the first to regularly assign priests to the region. I dwell on these arcane historical points because Bishop Kenrick was a major force in changing the structure of the Roman Catholic Church in America from that of a cooperative venture between laity and hierarchy to a monarchical structure in which the bishop owns all the assets and has absolute authority in his diocese. His zeal for central authority may have been a result of the controversy surrounding his consecration as bishop of Philadelphia. The lay trustees of St. Mary's church, which was the bishop's cathedral, refused to recognize him as pastor until he issued an interdict, the step just prior to excommunication. Few Catholics know that the church as originally established in America by John Carroll of Baltimore emulated the American system of democracy guided by mutual responsibility of laity and clergy. According to the East Coast author and theologian Anthony T. Padovano, Carroll's church was based on a trustee system with three characteristics:

- the laity nominates candidates as pastor and the bishop appoints
- the bishop has limited rights to dismiss a pastor
- disputes are settled in an arbitration committee, half of whose members are lay

Carroll himself refused to be appointed by Rome and insisted on an election by the clergy of his diocese. He was elected, of course. Parishes owned their own assets, which were administered by lay trustees elected by the parishioners. Other bishops were equally supportive of shared responsibility. Bishop John England of Charleston, SC, developed a "Constitution of the Roman Catholic Church of South Carolina," which noted that the bishop is not the "deputy of the Pope" any more than the governor of an American State is a deputy of the President of the United States.

That model did not sit well with Rome, which hoped to centralize all authority in the Vatican. In the mid-19th century, Bishop Kenrick and Archbishop John Hughes of New York led the charge in insisting that trustees be stripped of all power and ownership of all assets be transferred to the dioceses. Scranton's first bishop, William O'Hara, an Irish immigrant who had served under Kenrick, was appointed in 1869, bringing with him the central authority model espoused by his mentor. We will see that this had a role in the development of a persistent schism in South Scranton less than 30 years after Bishop O'Hara's arrival. Had the Carroll and England model persisted, one can speculate that there would be no Polish National Catholic Church today and the Roman church would not be embroiled in the current scandal over sexual abuse of children by predatory priests.

The city of Scranton was solidly working class—and solidly Democratic—with the Republican economic elite having long since fled to the suburbs. Good riddance! James T. Hanlon, a Democrat of course, was the mayor for so long that it almost seemed like an inherited office. As a child, I did not know a single Republican other than my uncle John Adams, who was such a nice guy it was hard to believe that he consorted with robber barons.

And while the economic conditions were constantly challenging, there many things of which we were proud as children growing up in the anthracite capital of the world. For one thing, we were the third largest city in Pennsylvania, pressed hard for than honor by Erie, which eventually surpassed us in population. For another, it was well known that we had the prettiest women in America, a fact confirmed regularly while strolling the sidewalks of the downtown commercial area. Downtown Scranton, which had been built on land reclaimed from a swamp, was rather ordinary, but two features stood out: the AM radio tower atop the Scranton Times Building at Penn Avenue and Spruce Street and the huge lighted sign flashing synchronously atop the Scranton Electric Building on Linden Street, proclaiming Scranton as "the Electric City." The claim was based on Scranton as the first city in America to build an electric streetcar system in the

1880s. The streetcars were still running during my childhood. And, there were the Scranton Red Sox, a Class A farm team of the Boston major league franchise of the same name. Baseball was a big deal in those days, when the NBA and NFL had many years to wait for their pre-eminence as spectator sports.

There was the Phoebe Snow, the famed Lackawanna Railroad train to New York, which whisked hundred of travelers daily to the terminal at Hoboken, just across the Hudson from Manhattan. And a new airport had been built at Avoca, midway between Scranton and Wilkes-Barre, officially Wilkes-Barre Scranton International Airport. Wilkes-Barre got top billing because the driving force behind development of the airport was Luzerne County Congressman Daniel J. Flood, who—like Mayor Hanlon—seemed to occupy an inherited position. It was said that Flood was so insistent on top billing for Wilkes-Barre that he would refuse to board a plane if the destination was announced as Scranton.

And even though the mining industry was responsible for scarring our landscape and littering it with piles of odoriferous burning culm, we were proud that anthracite was the best coal available, superior to soft bituminous coal mined in other parts of the country. We were grateful to have it to heat our homes and ship to other parts of the nation and the world.

That may seem like a particularly parochial view of the world, and it was. We had radio and newspapers, but no television, no 24-hour news channels to keep us abreast of what was going on in the world. We rarely traveled outside the valley and much less often outside the state. Metropolitan newspapers were available only at a few downtown newsstands or on Sunday when they were delivered to home subscribers. I never traveled to Philadelphia until I was in college and they opened the northeast extension of the Pennsylvania Turnpike, which made our state's largest city reasonably accessible. Those were different times and Scranton was all we had. We did our best to make the best of it.

2

Earliest Memories

My early childhood was spent in a two-story home at 500 North Blakely St. in Dunmore, a borough adjacent to the east side of Scranton. We lived on the second floor. Mother's cousin, Peg Brogan O'Hora, and her family lived on the first floor. Peg's husband, Edmund, was father's closest friend and worked with him in the post office.

My memories of Dunmore are limited, but some are quite vivid. My siblings, Edward and Ellen, the twins, were quite young at the time and kept Mother busy, giving me an opportunity to explore my limitations. I recall playing daily with my cousin, Anne O'Hora, in the back and side yards of our home, and I recall dimly that the neighbors, the McGlones, would sometimes complain of the noise we made. The back yard sloped up to an alley with a vacant lot on the other side, a lot where one day—wonder of wonders—a magnificent machine that we called a steam shovel appeared and began to clear the lot for construction. I was fascinated.

I also seem to recall a grape arbor in the back yard and some kind of sand box. Our second-floor back porch was made as child-proof as possible for the time, which I think meant there was no way I could wiggle through the railing and fall on my head.

I have two other memories of that time. Grandfather Edward McGuire often came to visit on the trolley, which meant he got off at the end of the line, a block to the south of our home. I would stand at the fence and watch him walking up Blakely Street. I have no recollection of what he looked like but remember that he always brought candy. He is the first person whose death I became aware of.

The other memory is of the practice air raids, which required us to draw heavy shades over all windows at night and be assured that air raid wardens were prowling the streets looking for dreaded Nazi bombers. At that stage in life, I was aware there was a war but had no appreciation for where it was or what it was all about. There had to be some discussion of it because I was also aware that Father had been turned down for enlistment because he had only one kidney. Also, I believe at the time he volunteered they were not taking men with families. At some point during the war I became aware that my Uncle Edward, Mother's brother, was serving as a physician with General Patton's army in Europe, wherever that was. Mother would get letters from him and try to hide from us that she was crying.

Before he went off to the war, Uncle Ed would take me out for a morning or afternoon drive to give Mother some relief. I suspect this occurred when he was home on vacation from medical school at St. Louis University. My most vivid memory of those escapades is of his hanging me out (Michael Jackson style) over the waters of Lake Scranton from the observation platform at the entrance to the lake. He wasn't trying to scare me, but it made an impression. In those days it was common for folks to drive around the lake on family outings. It was also common for young folks to park there at night, as evidenced by the proliferation of used prophylactics along the road. As we grew older I learned that young folks said they went there at night to watch the "boat races." Later, the water company closed the road but it remained popular with walkers. I also recall Uncle Ed's taking me to Philbin's gas station, where young men young men of the time congregated. Since gasoline was rationed during the war, I think we hung out more than we drove around. Philbin's livelihood probably depended more on soft drink and cigarette sales to idle young men than pumping gas.

My world was expanding, but at that point in my life it continued for the most part to be confined to the house and yard at 500 North Blakely.

Something I am aware of only through stories told in the family concern our parents' early days of marriage. Father got a coveted job in the post office through a competitive exam. It was the Depression and there was no work. He was one of the lucky ones. Mother had been a teacher but was required to resign after she married so that a family man could have that job. I learned years later that Mother prepared the same lunch every day for Father—a peanut butter any jelly sandwich.

The story is that he never took notice, but after several months his coworkers began to tease him for bringing the same lunch, day after day. It was no secret that food preparation was not one of Mother's passions or strengths, and this apparently was an early manifestation of that. I think it was also a manifestation of the fact Father did not demand varied or tantalizing meals. Meat and potatoes every night would have been fine. I suppose that is how he was able to stand 42 years in the post office and do it with a smile.

I can't say for sure when we moved from Dunmore to the Nativity section of Scranton, but it probably was sometime late in 1942 or early 1943. I don't remember any more air raid drills, so maybe by that time folks realized that Nazi bombers did not have the range to hit Scranton. I also don't know what occasioned the move, but it may have been prompted by Grandfather McGuire's death.

It was a wrenching experience. I knew there was more to the world than 500 North Blakely, but I had presumed I would live there for the rest of my life. I suppose the move made little impression on the twins, who were too young at that time to have put down any roots, but for me the move was devastating. Anne O'Hora was a person with whom I had an extraordinarily close relationship. I could not foresee how I could live without her.

In Nativity, the five of us lived in four rooms on the first floor of 222 Prospect Avenue. The kitchen and bathroom were in the rear with a door leading to a porch and the back yard. There was a hall leading to the two front rooms and a bedroom off the hall, where the children slept. It was a unisex dormitory. We lived there until I was 11 or 12, I believe, when we moved to our grandmother's quarters—10 rooms in all if you count the partially finished third floor—at 224 Prospect. It did not seem strange to me at the time, but Edward has noted that Grandmother Nellie McGuire must have been insensitive to Mother and our family in much smaller quarters next door.

The first peer I encountered after moving to Nativity was Bobby Naughton, my cousin, who lived next door. We met in the driveway that served the garage shared by our two houses. Bobby was older and most assuredly wiser in the ways of Nativity. He was also much stronger and more athletic than I, which became important when he nominated himself as responsible for "protecting" me and Edward from the roughnecks and bullies at Nativity School. I kept him busy because I quickly became a target and I did not know how to handle it on my own. I presume I was targeted because—then as now—I had trouble keeping my mouth shut when I thought I had something to say.

As we grew up, we never lacked supervision by adult relatives. Aunt Tessie Harrison and her husband, Uncle James, lived above us at 222. They had a lodger, a woman named Madge, who lived on the third floor, accessible only from Tessie's apartment. Bobby Naughton lived with his grandmother, our Aunt Kate Newcomb, his mother, Lucille, and his two sisters at 220 Prospect. The Walshes, relatives of our Father, lived next door on the other side at 226.

It is hard to say how old Nellie and Tessie and Kate were at the time. It's likely they were no older than I am today, but those were different times and they acted as though their lives were over. The only place they went was to Mass and to shop for food. Once in awhile Nellie would go for a car ride with us. Mostly, she sat in the front window and watched whatever was happening on Prospect Avenue, which was very little most of the time. I have since been told that Nellie lost interest in life when her oldest daughter, Ella Mae, died of peritonitis from a ruptured appendix—a clear case of medical malpractice if the facts recounted to me were at all accurate.

Kate and Tessie also spent a lot of time looking out the windows. That meant there was very little we children could get away with without being detected by one relative or another. That was frustrating for us, but must have provided comfort and security to mom and dad.

The house at 222-224 Prospect was heated by three coal-fired furnaces, which Mother called "boilers." Two of them required hand stoking from coal pails filled from bins at the other end of the cellar. The furnace on grandmother's side of the house had a large gravity-feed system that you filled daily with much finer anthracite than that used in the hand-fed furnaces. In later years Edward and I were given responsibilities for helping out with the furnace chores, a responsibility we resisted as much as we could.

The cellars on both sides of the house were mutually accessible, which helped a lot if you were feeding the furnaces. There was also accessibility on the second floor between grandmother's quarters and Tessie's apartment.

Prior to our moving from Dunmore to Nativity, I don't believe we visited often with the McGuires, since I don't recall meeting Aunt Tessie, Aunt Kate or the Naughtons until after we moved. However, I do remember very early visits with Father's parents—Thomas and Mary Walsh Carden. They lived at 213 South Irving Avenue, a home situated on a high lot with two flights of stairs leading to the front porch. Under the porch, I was to learn years later, was the hidden entrance to what apparently was operated as a speakeasy of sorts by my great-grandmother, the former Mary Gerrity, who was left with five young children after the untimely demise of Ter(r)ence—one or two Rs, take your pick—our great-grandfather. I will save the story of his mysterious life and death for later.

I did not learn the story of the "tavern" until many years later. It reportedly had been operated surreptitiously by Mary after Terence's death, and the tavern fixtures reportedly were still in the cellar under the porch. Perhaps that is why my early memories of the cellar, accessed from inside the home by a set of stairs from the kitchen, are of a dark mysterious place into which I was reluctant to venture. It was the place into which Father disappeared one day in my later childhood to emerge with his old baseball mitt—a subject I will explore in detail later as well.

When we visited Thomas and Mary Carden, my memories are that we generally sat in the kitchen, perhaps because there was a coal stove there and it was the main heat source in the house. There was central heating, but it was less expensive to heat the kitchen with the coal stove and spend most of your time there, allowing you to burn less coal in the furnace.

Other than the coal stove, I recall the GE refrigerator in the kitchen—one of the early models with the condenser on top. From that refrigerator Grandmother Carden invariably retrieved a cold bottle of milk and poured a glass to slake my thirst. What I remember was that it was a robust glass of milk, clinging to the sides of the glass. Fat-free milk it was not. Like most refrigerators, the GE kept running and running and will still operable when Grandfather Carden died years later. It was somewhat remarkable because many folks living in Nativity at the time did not have refrigerators. I was to learn that when we moved there and I encountered the ice man making deliveries to Grandmother McGuire and my other relatives. The ice was harvested from lakes in the winter and delivered regularly all year. People kept food in "ice boxes," which were large insulated cabinets with drains for the ice melt. Obviously, this was before the time of frozen foods.

I really haven't thought much until now about why my recollections of early vis-its were with the Cardens and not the McGuires. One possible explanation is that our family and the Cardens shared ownership of a 1941 Chevy, which was housed in the garage at the at the back of the lot at 213 South Irving. The Chevy was a source of contention for our Mother, which I will explore later in this tale. Another possible explanation is that in those early days it may have been that just as Uncle Ed took me out from time to time to give Mother a break, Father did the same. And since gas was rationed, visiting mom and dad was probably the best option available to him. Since the twins were very young at that time, he and I made these excursions alone.

3

Elementary School

Shortly after the move from Dunmore, I embarked on an experience that was formative—school, kindergarten to be precise. We Carden children all attended Nativity of Our Lord School, one block up Hemlock Street from the family home. The parish was the center of our lives: school five days a week, daily Mass, Bingo on Friday nights where Father worked as a volunteer, religious festivals throughout the year and on and on.

Nativity was a close-knit neighborhood where everyone seemed to know everyone else. This was particularly vexing for us children, for we could go nowhere without having folks who knew us report to our parents if we strayed from neighborhood behavioral expectations. Nativity was an Irish-German ghetto of sorts. The majority of families were of Irish descent. Mother never stressed our Irish heritage—possibly, I was to learn later, because she may have been embarrassed by the raw behavior of some neighbors who were immigrants. Nevertheless, Mother apparently subliminally identified with the Irish, because she was in the habit of asking, "What kind of name is that?" when one of us mentioned an acquaintance with an unfamiliar-sounding name. Father seemed to identify more strongly with his Irish heritage and often attended the annual Friendly Sons of St. Patrick dinner.

Aside from the Irish majority, there were plenty of families of German descent and children with German names in the parish school. And there were some children in the neighborhood whose families identified more closely with their German heritage. They went to St. Mary's, a neighboring German ethnic parish. During the war, we were too young to notice if there were any tensions between the two populations.

Another neighboring parish, Sacred Heart, was where the children of Polish descent went to school. We did not encounter any of them because there were few Polish families known to be living in Nativity. We were aware of them, however, because the Immaculate Heart of Mary nuns told dark and scary tales about Sacred Heart, where the pastor was an auxiliary bishop, appointed in the wake of a terrible heretical schism by a young Polish priest who formed his own church. The heresy, as I came to learn later, was that the priest, Francis (actually, Francizek) Hodur, an immigrant from Poland, founded the Polish National Catholic Church after parishioners of Sacred Heart rioted in 1896 over their lack of control of the use of parish funds or consultation in the assignment of priests. They wanted Polish-speaking priests to serve their Polish-speaking congregation, which does not seem to be an unrealistic expectation.

The following year, Father Hodur founded St. Stanislaus Bishop & Martyr Parish, based on several principles, including legal ownership of parish properties by the parishioners and requiring approval by parishioners in the assignment of priests. Father Hodur envisioned that Polish bishops would be appointed by Rome with the advice and consent of the parishioners. As we have seen, it is ironic that these powers had been granted to the laity in the church model established by America's first bishop, John Carroll. They had been revoked less than 50 years earlier when Rome balked at the American model for organizing and administering the church. Father Hodur and his followers did not consider themselves heretics, but that did not prevent his excommunication by the Diocese of Scranton, which had ordained him, in 1898. The split was irrevocable and Father Hodur demonstrated his contempt for the Roman church by burning the excommunication documents and throwing the ashes in a nearby brook, according to the official history of his church.

In subsequent years, Father Hodur was elected bishop by his followers and later was consecrated a bishop by the Old Catholic Church in Holland, which had been formed in the wake of Vatican I by Catholics who refused to accept Pius IX's claim of papal infallibility, endorsed reluctantly by the church council. That consecration ensured apostolic succession—a principle related to the claim of an unbroken chain of authority from the original apostles to modern bishops. Bishop Hodur was still alive during my childhood. He died in 1953 and his church now claims 25,000 members in parishes throughout the United States and Canada—five in Chicago alone.

I have outlined this memory in some detail because it is the single instance I recall from my childhood of being taught hatred and intolerance. Our nuns simply could not contemplate any mere mortal challenging the unquestioned authority of Holy Mother the Church. They demonized Bishop Hodur as a heretic and worse. I was convinced as a young child that he had to be an agent of Satan, patron of evil, a concept I accepted unquestioningly at that age. The nuns certainly had no sympathy for his insistence on meaningful lay participation in the governance of parishes, an issue that has arisen again in the wake of the terrible scandal of sexual abuse of children by priests aided and abetted by their bishops. The Polish National cathedral in South Scranton, St. Stanislaus, is named for the same saint as the Polish Roman Catholic Church in St. Louis that is currently defying the archbishop there by refusing to turn over the deed to their parish property. It seems that despite their individual piety, at least some Polish Christians are not about to be pushed around by the Roman hierarchy. Good for them! They deserve support from the rest of us who are disillusioned by the bishops' enablement and cover-up of sexual abuse of children by predator priests.

Perhaps the reason we were shielded from the intolerance that marked so much of the nation at that time is that there was little diversity in our community. While we were well aware of the "evil" on our southern border, it might as well have been on a different continent for all it mattered to us children. Theoretically it was a terrible situation and gave the nuns something to obsess about. But all children and all families we regularly encountered were the same as our own and those of our friends. We often visited in the homes of our friends and rarely experienced anything unfamiliar. I should add that our friends did not often visit in our home because Mother did not want them hanging around our house. Perhaps it was because of the crowded conditions in the four rooms (Actually three, since we were not allowed to use the front room except on special occasions. It was the classic example of the "good parlor," which may be a peculiarly Scranton concept.).

There were virtually no children of other ethnic derivations in the parish. I recall when an Italian family moved into a small house just west of the school on Hemlock Street. The grandfather, who apparently came from the "old country," had a vegetable garden that the young Irish-German thugs of Nativity loved to raid. The old man would run out of the house and chase the boys down the street, but either was too slow to catch them or just wanted to run them off. I did not participate in these escapades because I was sure he would catch me if I did and I knew that Father would make me pay twice for the transgression.

Ralph Falzetti, the old man's grandson, was a classmate of mine. He was the only child in that house. There was no father. It is unclear to me now whether he had been killed in the war or simply left the family. Life for Ralph was difficult. Nearly every school day as classes were breaking for lunch, male classmates cornered Ralph in the "cloak room" (an unexplained designation since no one wore cloaks) and administered corporal punishment. His transgression was that he was different. This was the first time I encountered such behavior.

I have vivid memories of the ritual. Ralph would stand in the corner of the small room at the back of the classroom, flanked by the two larger boys. They asked him to tense his abdomen and pulled up his shirt to feel the abdominal wall. Ralph had visible abdominal muscles, which was fortunate because the boys took turns punching him in the abdomen, calling out, "Let's see if the guinea can take it." Ralph took it—day after day. It did not seem to affect him physically but I have no idea the emotional price he paid. And for what? Being different. I can say that we were never taught prejudice against any ethnic group—either at home or in school. But the nuns had to know this was going on. Were it an Irish or German boy, they would have stepped in immediately. What I did not understand at the time is that children can be cruel and if unsupervised or unchecked by responsible adults they are capable of unspeakable behavior. Eventually, the bullies tired of the ritual and Ralph was accepted as one of us. His sunny disposition and engaging smile certainly helped.

I don't want to give the impression that all the boys at Nativity were bullies, but those I describe as thugs were considered mainstream by my classmates. I can't speak for the experience of Edward and Ellen, who were two years behind me, but it could not have been substantially different. On the other hand, the three Carden children **were** different. Our parents expected not only that we would finish high school but would go on to college. They often reminded us that they were both college graduates, which was most unusual at that time and place. On the other hand, they seemed to have little if any sympathy for the position that put us in. We were expected to excel in our schoolwork and not concern ourselves with the wasteful pursuits of our peers. I presume that from the perspective of those peers, we were rejecting their values—and those of their parents, who, by and large, were not educated and saw no reason their children should be. They did not appreciate our "enlightenment," which I for one was somewhat uncertain of at the time. I have no recollection that either Mother or Father taught us that we were inherently superior to our peers. However, there was no doubt we were expected to perform better than they did academically.

It was not easy being different. If it were not for the protection of Bobby Naughton, who was perfectly capable of standing up to any of our peers my life would have been much worse. As it was, there were plenty of unpleasant encounters. Bobby not only protected me, he was involved in several of the milestones in my life. He taught me to swim in Roaring Brook and saved my life when I was carried off by the current. Later, he taught me to drive when he bought his first car, a 1937 floor-shift Plymouth. Since he could not buy a car until he was 16 and since I was 13 in eighth grade, he apparently was at least three years older than I but only a year ahead of me in school.

As we progressed though Nativity School an issue arose over where we would attend high school. A new Catholic high school had opened on the border between Nativity and Sacred Heart Parishes. Father Collins, a favorite of Father and Mother, was principal and he lived at the Nativity rectory. I took advantage of an unexpected opportunity to join the South Scranton Catholic High School marching band when I was in the seventh grade and soon was "first saxophone." My expectation was that I and my siblings would go to South Catholic, as it was known. They had a football team and I wanted to play football.

Mother made it clear, however, that it was my destiny to go to Scranton Prep, the Jesuit high school downtown—a possibility that had never entered my head up to that point. Prep did not have a football team and I knew nothing about it. It may not have been easy at Nativity, but at least I knew where I stood, and nothing was expected to change at South Catholic, where, after all, I was a member of the marching band—hot stuff for a seventh grader. Prep had an entrance exam and awarded scholarships based on performance in that exam. Both Edward and I won partial scholarships. That was a big deal. Our names were published in the daily newspapers, which served to create more expectations of high academic performance.

Where we went to high school made a difference. Of the 50-some children in my eighth grade class, five boys went to college after high school. Several girls entered the convent. Presumably, most of them were sent to college if they stayed in. A

Lebanese girl, Jemella Abdella, (a real outlier for Nativity) went on to Marywood Seminary and College. Other than that, I know of no other girls who went on to college. Of the five boys who went to college, four of us graduated from Scranton Prep and only one from South Catholic, where most of the children from Nativity went to high school. Two of Edward's grade school classmates went to Prep and I recall only one girl, Mary Greta Bird, accompanying Ellen to Marywood Seminary. She later went into the convent, where she remains to this day, I am told. The parents of all collegians shared values similar to those of our parents. Interestingly, I have no ongoing relationship with any of the other children who shared eight years of elementary education with me. I think the same was true of Ellen and Edward. When we returned to Scranton for Father's funeral, one girl from my elementary school class, Janeanne Nealon O'Boyle came to the viewing.

She had been the first love of my life.

4

A Parish Defines a Neighborhood

A good deal of this discussion has centered on Nativity—the neighborhood and the school. Nativity was the only neighborhood in Scranton to be named for a Roman Catholic parish. It is not uncommon in major cities for ethnic populations to be identified with parishes and parishes to define neighborhoods. But in my experience it is uncommon for a neighborhood to be named for the parish.

I suppose Nativity is an improvement from "Shanty Hill"—*Ben seanti* in Gaelic—the original name for the neighborhood across Roaring Brook and up the hill from the railroad right-of-way and the Lackawanna Iron & Steel Works. It was called Shanty Hill because the original homes there were considered shacks, the homes of the poor laborers in the steel furnaces. Many of the workers apparently were Irish Catholic because the first Mass in Scranton was celebrated in Shanty Hill in 1840 at 522 Front Street, overlooking Roaring Brook, according to parish records. It was the most populous neighborhood in Scranton in the mid-19th century. The railroad was the Delaware, Lackawanna and Western, where Grandfather McGuire had been employed as a steam locomotive engineer. He could walk to work across either the Spruce Street or Cedar Avenue Bridge.

While the neighborhood was ordinary by any standard I can think of, it was dominated by one magnificent structure, the church of the Nativity of Our Lord, which stood proudly at the intersection of Orchard Street and South Webster Avenue, one block east of our home. The church had been built, I was told often as a child, by the legendary Reverend Doctor John J. Loughran, a priest bigger than life who apparently prowled his parish domain looking for miscreants to whom he could express his displeasure by whacking them with his cane. The church apparently had been constructed in stages, starting with what we called the "lower church" at ground level and later the imposing "upper church" with its huge dome adorned with paintings of biblical scenes and impressive stained glass windows in the rear and both sides. Existence of the lower church provided flexibility and allowed a full schedule of Masses during the war when coal was scarce and the upper church was difficult to heat. It was also the location of the dreaded confessionals that became part of our weekly ritual later in childhood.

The good doctor was "dead and gone," as they used to say in Scranton, when we moved to Nativity. He had reigned from 1907 to 1940. It was not only the political offices in Scranton that seemed to be awarded in perpetuity. But the church lived on. As a child, I found it to be an inspiring structure—much more impressive architecturally than poor old St. Peter's Cathedral on Wyoming Avenue downtown. And we had plenty of opportunity to appreciate its magnificence.

Daily Mass was part of the routine. We sat with our classmates, supervised by the nuns, who had a habit of creeping up on you and pinching you for any transgression—real or imagined—during the sacred ritual. It seems we were never devout enough to totally resist the many distractions that deter children from complete immersion in the sublime.

Then there were the endless religious holidays and festivals, many of which involved processions. The altar boys were bedecked in black cassocks with white surplices and the choir boys in white cassocks with short red, gold-tinged capes. If girls were allowed in the procession they wore white dresses and veils. My recollection that most processions—as with most things in the church—were reserved for the chosen gender as defined by the presence of a y chromosome. An exception, of course, was the May celebration in honor of the unsullied Mother of Jesus.

I was in the choir. I believe Edward was, too, but am not sure. There were no girls in the choir, but there were adult women. What I am sure of is that we did not have a choice. Sister Victoire, who taught music and I believe second grade, made the infallible determination of whose angelic voice was necessary for the greater glory of God. There was no mechanism for appeal. It did not matter that I would have preferred to be an altar boy. I was terribly disappointed since the choir performed mostly in a loft at the rear of the church while the altar boys participated in the sacred rite in the sanctuary at the front of the church. Processions were the exception and I looked forward to them.

Eventually I got my chance to serve as an altar boy and never looked back. I learned the Latin in a week and proudly donned my cassock and surplice, never again to be relegated to the choir loft in the back of the church. I was up front in the sanctuary where I belonged. Serving Mass was something I enjoyed, particularly since it conveyed certain privileges. If you served a funeral mass it meant you did not have to be in school. And if you were selected to go to the cemetery for the graveside service, your hiatus from the classroom was extended, so much the better. Solemn high funeral Masses required at least three altar boys, so there was a very good chance of being scheduled to serve at least once a week. The lead altar boy for a solemn high mass was known as the master of ceremonies. He carried the crucifix at the head of the procession up and down the aisle before and after Mass. At a funeral Mass. he stood at the foot of the casket, opposite the priest, for the final blessings. I particularly remember serving as master of ceremonies for the funeral Mass of my Grandmother Carden, who died in 1951 when I was in eighth grade.

The liturgy in those pre-Vatican II days was the Tridentine Mass, which dated to the Council of Trent. Only the Sunday readings of Scripture to the congregation and the homily or sermon were in English. Otherwise, the entire ceremony was in Latin. The priest intoned a prayer and the altar boys responded on cue.

In nomine Patris, et Filii, et Spiritus Sancti, the priest opened.

Amen, we responded.

Introibo ad altare Dei.

Ad Deum qui laetificat juventutem meam. And so it went.

No one thought to ask whether the folks in the pews had any idea what these prayers meant in English. It was not considered important. We children were encouraged to buy daily missals with English on one side of the page and Latin on the other. Other than the children, few of the congregation had missals. As I sat in the sanctuary, particularly during daily mass, I saw clusters of what seemed to be mostly elderly women scattered about the church. Most wore dark clothes, and covered their bowed heads with scarves, known as babushkas. Most prayed the rosary rather than following the ceremony taking place on the altar. Grandmother McGuire was prominent among them, sitting about a quarter of the way back on the left hand side of the church facing the altar. In a sense, we and the priest were actors on a ecclesial stage and the congregation was the audience, but neither seemed to take much notice of the other. The only exception was at the communion when the few folks who considered themselves worthy came to the altar rail where the priest placed a consecrated host on their tongues. Those who came forward surely demonstrated confidence in the state of their immortal souls, since the prayer immediately before communion, *Domine non sum dignus,* clearly declared them unworthy.

The parish property consisted of four architecturally consistent stone buildings. The rectory just west of the church housed anywhere from four to five priests, served by a staff that included a cook and housekeeper. Those days are long gone. The parish was supported by the weekly offertory collection and the Friday Bingo, which attracted folks from as far away as Binghamton, N.Y. and Hazleton, south of Wilkes-Barre.

The convent was north of the church at the intersection of South Webster Avenue and Hemlock Street. It had been built on the site of the first Catholic church in Scranton, which opened in 1847. The convent was attached to the school through what we called a "cloister," which allowed to nuns to come and go from the school without the necessity of being exposed to the profane secular world. My recollection is that there were 10 or so nuns who staffed the school. We had no lay teachers. Since there were nine grades, including kindergarten, there were at least nine nuns. I can't recall if the principal, Mother Benigna, IHM—perhaps better described as Mother Maligna—was assigned to a class or merely filled in if one of the other nuns was sick.

The school was an equally imposing three-story stone structure. I believe it was the last of the parish buildings to be constructed. It had a grand entrance with a kitchen and cloak room, as well as an auditorium that took up most of the first floor. The auditorium was the site of school assemblies, but more importantly it provided a home for the all-important Nativity Bingo. Floors in the school were of marble blocks about three feet square, separated by thin strips of brass. When it was time for lunch or for dismissal for the day, the nuns had each class line up in the halls along the brass strips and await their signal to march briskly but silently out of the school to "The Stars and Stripes Forever" or some other John Philip Sousa classic, played over the public address system.

Our nuns were from the dominant Catholic order in Scranton—Sisters, Servants of the Immaculate Heart of Mary—which had its local headquarters at Marywood in the Green Ridge Section of town. In later years we speculated that IHM really meant "I Hate Men," but while we were in school we never thought to make fun of them because they were clearly a formidable force in their dark blue habits and white wimples, a force not to be trifled with. This was particularly true for the Carden children. We all knew that if a nun disciplined us and our parents found out it could mean additional discipline or at a minimum an endorsement of the nun's judgment. In our house, the teacher was always right.

While the nuns may or may not have hated men, they certainly hated sex—or seemed to. "Take your hands out of your pocket, mister" was a command commonly issued long before any one of us was old enough to "invent" masturbation (many children who discover their libido in this manner are convinced initially that they have invented the maneuver). Perhaps they feared that proximity of the hands to the genitals in and of itself would speed up the discovery and lead the irascible into the perdition of mortal sin. To be fair to the nuns and their neuroses, I do not recall the girls ever being cautioned to avoid patent leather shoes. Maybe there were limits to the IHM erotiphobia.

Aside from the church, the Nativity neighborhood was quite ordinary. In fact, all along the 200 block of South Webster Avenue across from the parish property stood some fairly decrepit commercial and residential structures. The classiest piece of property on the block was Golden's drugstore, which was next to a barber shop at South Webster and Orchard. At South Webster and Hemlock, across from the convent, was Merrick's, the equivalent of which today would be a convenience store. Merrick's was a hangout for neighborhood boys. I loved to go there and play the pinball machine, but that was not one of the privileges Mother and Father allowed. Not to worry, there was always a chance for a few surreptitious games after choir practice. At a nickel a game, I could not afford much more than that.

In the middle of the block stood a grocery story, a creepy place that gave me the impression it was an incubator for pestilence. The store was crowded and dark, nothing like the open aisles at the local Acme and A&P "super markets" where Mother shopped. It was a remnant of an earlier time when all shopping was done at neighborhood markets. In fact, when we moved to Nativity there was a small A&P and an independent butcher shop in a residential-commercial building at the corner of Prospect and Orchard, next to the Walsh family home. These small markets remained in business by offering things the "super markets" did not—home delivery and groceries on credit. Mother needed neither, since she paid cash for everything and had competent—if unenthusiastic—labor to provide delivery. What was my little red wagon for if not to schlep down to the Acme and bring back the week's groceries? Even the big outfits provided some home sales and delivery. A&P had a station wagon seen often in the neighborhood delivering tea—after all it was a tea company—and, perhaps coffee to residential customers.

The neighborhood A&P was managed by a neighbor, Tony Mangan, whose grandson was in Edward and Ellen's class at Nativity School. In Nativity, everyone knew everyone else. The corner A&P closed when the Great Atlantic and Pacific Tea Company opened a "super market" on Pittston Avenue two blocks south of the Globe Theater, where we attended the matinee showing almost every Saturday at a cost of 12 cents. In those days before television, there were serial adventure presentations called "chapters," and Movietone News, in addition to the feature film, which almost inevitably was a western with Roy Rogers or Gene Autry or whoever.

Daily deliveries were made also by the local dairies. Woodlawn used panel trucks, but Burschel's still used horses and wagons. The milk was different then, too. No one drank "skim" milk. You had the choice of homogenized milk, known today as whole milk, or traditional milk with the heavy cream at the neck of the bottle. Most folks got the traditional milk—saving a penny a bottle—and distributed the cream through the milk by inverting the bottle multiple times. At one point during our childhood, Mother discovered powdered milk. She would mix the powder with water and add a portion of cream saved from the traditional milk. We definitely preferred "real milk" to the "blue milk" produced from powder.

Population density in the neighborhood was high. Our grandparents had lived initially in what had been steel company employee housing on Prospect Avenue. I am not sure what level of employees had lived in the homes, but they certainly were a cut above other employee housing remnants in the neighborhood. Nellie and Edward McGuire and Kate and Tom Newcomb had purchased what amounted to a twin home (Philadelphia term), sawed it in half to make two homes and moved the two small homes to the back of their lots, adjacent to the alley.

On the front of the lots the families both erected large homes facing Prospect Avenue. I have described the home in which we grew up. The Newcomb home was of different design—living quarters for individual families or tenants on each of three floors. All along our street there were homes at the back and front of most lots—a pattern that was seen throughout the neighborhood. Homes were no more than 10 feet from each other, leaving room for a path from front to back or—as with our home and Newcombs'—for two homes to share a driveway.

At the back of each lot was an alley—designated officially as a "court" on maps of the community. No one called them courts; they were alleys. The alley network was well known to all children. Sometimes there were interconnecting alleys. For instance, behind our property was an alley running north-south. Just to the north of our property it intersected with an east-west alley that in turn intersected with another north-south alley behind the properties on the east side of the 200 block of Pittston Avenue. In our early years we used to alley network as we walked to the Saturday matinee at the Globe Theater. Among our friends were the children of the Giles family who lived on the alley behind the 300 block of Prospect Avenue. We and they walked the alleys to meet and play. In the winter, there were certain alleys appropriated for sledding. Parents always knew we were safe sledding under controlled conditions and the watchful eyes of other parents. Years later, we sometimes thoughtlessly raced the cars we had so recently learned to drive through these narrow, unpaved thoroughfares, causing no end of annoyance, I am sure. But teen-agers are not known for their sensitivity.

All in all, Nativity may have been ordinary, but it had a magnificent church, of which we all were extraordinarily proud, and seemed to offer everything we could possibly need.

5

Finding Something to Do

Preparing descriptions of the environment in which we lived as children raises the question in my mind why we remember some things and forget others. I think it is clear that we remember those things that we perceive as having affected us personally—disputes, conflict, nurturing events. Therefore, I explain my lack of detailed memories of our early sibling relationships as a result of my perception that our early childhood experiences occurred in a sea of tranquility. Among the tranquil memories I have is of playing barber with father as he sat reading the newspaper. I would pretend to cut his hair—what little he had—while making a buzzing sound with my mouth. How he could concentrate on the news remains a mystery to me. That is just one example of the simplicity of life at the time. I recall no conflict or tension in the home, no jealousies or disputes. I doubt there was a complete absence of normal sibling rivalry, but I have no recollection of the details.

For instance, I noted earlier that all three of us slept in a single bedroom adjacent to the kitchen at 222 Prospect. I have very little recollection of that room. I can't even recall for certain how the beds were laid out. I have only two specific memories of that room. One was when the twins were thought to have whooping cough. I remember the persistent, brassy, hacking cough and the makeshift mist tents over the beds. I don't know if there was a doctor in attendance or even if it was whooping cough, since I presume *pertussis* vaccine was available at that time. I also presume I remember it because it was clear that the illness was serious and could result in disastrous consequences for one or both of my siblings.

The other memory is of an illness of unknown nature that confined me to bed in that room for an extended period—a week or so. Mother provided me with a translation of the *Odyssey*, which I read through while confined to bed. Since I could not pronounce the Greek names I simply jumped over them as I read. I had no idea at the time that it was a great classic of western literature.

Life for children at that time was extraordinarily unchallenging. There was a whole lot of nothin' goin' on. It was bad enough for little boys, but must have been terrible for little girls—something that escaped my notice at the time. In those early years it was rare for any of us to venture outside the two-square-block area that encompassed Nativity parish and our home—other than Saturday trips to the Globe Theater for the 12-cent matinee.

One thing little boys could do was play marbles. We drew circles in the dirt and played with Bobby Naughton. Sometimes Edward and I would play on the rug at home. Edward and I had the advantage that we could go out to play with Bobby and Mother felt secure. Ella—as she was known then—had to entertain herself at home much of the time. I seem to recall that little girls gathered in each others' homes, but, as we've already seen, Mother discouraged that.

We have to remember that it was a time and a place where women were expected to become housewives. Ella, also known as Ella Mae in remembrance of her dead aunt, was expected to become an educated housewife, meaning that she was expected to finish college but follow the tradition of forsaking a career for home and family. This was ironic, of course, since Mother clearly resented that she had been forced to resign as a teacher on being married. But married women in Scranton at that time rarely worked outside the home.

I recall that our weekday routine was uneventful. We had to wait for Father to exit the single bathroom before we would get ready for school. He was obsessive about his routine, the predictability of which apparently contributed enough strength for him to face the day. Since he walked to work, he left early and we took over the bathroom. Mother always made our breakfasts, which often consisted of bacon and eggs with toast, something Father would have been satisfied to have for breakfast every day of his life.

We spent the day in school for three-quarters of the year, coming home for lunch, which was equally unmemorable. After school, there was little to do other than whatever homework was assigned. We looked forward to the radio serials in the late afternoon. We hated to miss a single episode of the Lone Ranger or Sky King. The afternoon newspaper "funnies" also occupied some of our time.

As I said, there was a whole lot of nothin' goin' on. By contrast, it seems to me as one observing the current generation that children today have the opportunity to participate in an endless variety of organized activities both in school and the community. This was not true in the Nativity and the late 1940s and early '50s. There was no Little League or Pop Warner football and absolutely no intramural programs at the school. I believe that was typical for the time. There were no dance classes or soccer programs for the girls either. I don't think any of us had ever heard of soccer.

As we grew older, there was no tennis or golf. I can remember only one family in Nativity whose children played golf. That was the Whelans, whose Father was the local general practitioner. Boys had considerably more options than girls. We were eligible for exploitation by the local newspaper publishers who had been made exempt by Congress from the child labor laws so that children could disseminate their product throughout the community at an acceptable cost. Congress apparently believed—or was persuaded by the publishers' lobby—that it was a good thing for young men to learn "business skills and values" at a young age. That it was profitable for the publishers never entered their minds, I am certain.

Both Edward and I had multiple paper routes—serving at various times the morning paper, The Scranton Tribune, and the afternoon paper, The Times. I seem to recall that for some time we shared an afternoon route and both of us were fired when neither showed up one day. And there was the Sunday paper route. In that activity, we worked for the Anthracite News Service, which had a contract to deliver the Sunday paper, The Scrantonian, as well as the New York and Philadelphia Sunday papers. That was our first venture into entrepreneurship, since we had to pay for every paper we delivered and were obliged to collect from the subscribers if we were to realize the profit. It was amazing how some folks dodged payment for weeks at a time. It never occurred to us at the time that we were being exploited by the publishers and distributors who got paid whether we did or not.

While there were numerous benefits to the paper routes, particularly in the degree of independence and lack of need for reliance on what had been meager family allowances, the work was not fun. It was hard to face the prospect of leaving a warm bed on a cold, dark winter morning to deliver the day's news to the front doors of ungrateful subscribers. On some occasions when we were under the weather, Mother would drive us on our morning paper routes, but that service was not routinely available. Bundles of morning papers were delivered to our porch, but we had to go downtown to the formidable Times Building to obtain our daily allocation for delivery of the afternoon paper.

We gathered in a dingy anteroom between the press room and the mail room and the product was carried on a conveyor belt across the ceiling and down to the tables where the circulation workers bound them in bundles for the waiting trucks or counted them out for us. We filed, one-by-one, through a "cage" and waited at a window where the circulation workers literally threw our allocation into our waiting arms. On heavy advertising days, particularly during the Christmas holiday season, the papers were too big to fit in the heavy cloth bags we had been issued to carry them. On those occasions, we left The Times Building with a full bag on one shoulder and carrying a bundle of papers with one or both arms.

We carried our load two blocks east to Washington Avenue and Spruce Street where we boarded a trolley for the Hill Section, where our delivery route began. The daily allocation included an extra paper for the streetcar motorman, who obligingly provided free passage. There was also a "free" paper for home use. On Friday evenings as we delivered the papers and again on Saturday mornings we made the rounds, trying to collect. The Times kept track of subscriber bills and provided us with receipts to be handed over in exchange for payment. Some afternoon subscribers were as evasive as those of the morning and Sunday papers. We had exposure to deadbeats at an early age, but at least we were not on the hook for those who did not pay.

While Edward and I both were involved in newspaper delivery, this was not true of most of our classmates. I don't know what they did with their afternoons or mornings. As we have discussed, by and large, they were not the ambitious sort. It is not clear why we were, since I don't recall either Mother or Father urging us to take on this outside work. I do recall that at an early age I began to help a local boy who had a paper route. He paid me a pittance and I schlepped around Nativity with him. Maybe it provided a sense of purpose. More likely the pittance was attractive at that age.

I do recall that as earnings from the paper routes became "substantial" for that time and our age, Father wanted to help us with financial "management." In other words, he wanted us to turn over the earnings, which he would manage so we could not spend them. That became a source of friction, which led me to develop all sorts of skills in passive resistance. Neither Father nor Mother was enamored with spending money and I felt that was why it had been invented.

Revenue from the paper routes gave me and Edward a desired level of independence. Maybe that was important to us because we were so closely supervised by our parents, something not true for the bulk of our classmates. Unfortunately, this option was not open to Ellen. Another advantage we enjoyed was great mobility once we learned to ride bicycles. Our first bike was a hand-me-down from John Adams, but it was a great liberation device. Bobby Naughton and I would ride together all over the neighborhood and beyond. As I grew older, the forays became bolder. I know that we rode up the Moosic Street hill to Lake Scranton and around the Lake from time to time. I can also remember riding to Rocky Glen, the area amusement park in Moosic—quite a trek for a young boy.

Mostly, we rode in the summer to South Scranton Junior High School, where there was a rudimentary playground of sorts behind the school. By today's standards, it was pretty pathetic, but there were very few recreational facilities available to us. There was Harmon Field south east of Stafford Avenue near the current River Street exit off I-81. Since we had no organized team sports, that facility was essentially useless to us. I can also remember gathering with other boys from Nativity on a dirt field next to the dump (excuse me—waste disposal facility) east of Stafford Avenue to play touch football. I liked to play center and thought I would play that position in high school. In later years that property was developed as a retail center with an A&P store where I worked while in high school and college.

We also spent a great deal of time wandering the land along the Laurel Line tracks on the south side of Roaring Brook, all the way east to Nay Aug where we crossed the brook on the pedestrian bridge to the park. Nay Aug had a huge municipal pool where we spent a lot of time in the summers. I can still remember how shocking it was to change into swimming trunks in a room full of strangers. I guess I had lived a fairly sheltered existence no matter how much I considered myself a man of the world.

A more intimate swimming facility was operated by the city in South Side, on the far fringes of our neighborhood. We would walk there with Bobby in time to be in the water when it opened at 8 A.M. It was what would be known today as an Olympic-sized pool with two diving boards, the most challenging of which was a high board. It took a lot of courage for me to climb the ladder to the platform, make my way out what appeared at the time to be an extremely narrow board to the end before jumping into the water below. Eventually, I learned to dive from the high platform.

Had Mother been aware of this, she probably would have been frantic. Mother was extraordinarily courageous about some things but extraordinarily timid in her fears for her family. She always saw the dark side of every situation—the potential harm that could befall a loved one. Perhaps this was a residuum of the death of her sister, which neither she nor her mother ever got over, it seems.

I would not have been swimming at all were it not for Aunt Tessie. Bobby wanted to take me swimming and I wanted to go in the worst way, but Mother would not approve. Tessie jumped in on one of these conversations. "Jean, let him go. Boys have to be boys. It will be all right. It's time he learned to swim." Tessie prevailed and I learned to swim. Swimming at Nay Aug and South Side pools was one thing, but I am sure Mother would not have approved of our swimming in Roaring Brook. It was reputed to have been polluted with unspeakable filth. But Roaring Brook was open when the city pools were closed, so we went there often in the spring. A favorite sport was jumping from the rocks adjacent to the falls just under the Nay Aug pedestrian bridge into the pool below. Some boys dove into the pool, but I never gained a sufficient degree of confidence that my head would not slam into a hidden rock below. I felt that my legs and butt could sustain such a calamity without permanent damage. While it provided great fun, Roaring Brook almost got the best of me. One day while swimming in a pool above the Nay Aug Falls, I was carried off by the current. Bobby jumped in the water and grabbed me, undoubtedly saving my life. We did not tell Mother of that experience and she never mentioned it. Recently my daughter, Andrea, informed me that her grandmother told her the story several times, so it is clear she knew more than it appeared.

Roaring Brook was also the setting for occasional encounters with children from The Flats, an area south of downtown and west of Nativity. We did not really know any of these children but the impression was that they were uniformly bad actors of whom we had to be wary. The Flats was considered a slum. It was a mixture of industrial and run-down residential properties. I don't recall ever really getting to know any of the children we encountered. I suppose they were equally wary of us.

6

The Great Misadventure

Roaring Brook and the land along the Laurel Line tracks south of the river was the setting for the one great misadventure of my early years. In the spring of 1948 when I was in fourth grade, Father was called to the convent with me to be told by Sister Phillipa, IHM, a veritable bear of a woman, that I had defaced my binder (bought and paid for by me or my parents) with ink from the inkwell on my desk. I was fascinated that the ink oxidized on contact with air and dried with a metallic sheen. I'm sure the good nun never asked herself why I was so bored with whatever she was teaching that I had to find something to amuse myself. So, it was with trepidation that I accompanied Father up Hemlock Street to the convent. We were shown into a small sitting room and met with Sister Phillipa. I have no recollection of what was said, what terribly sinister conclusion she had reached about my behavior, but I dreaded most what would happen afterward. It was clear in our house that the nuns were always right and we would be held accountable for any transgressions in school.

As Father and I were walking home, he did not comment on the merits of the issue, but merely said, "I never want to have to come back here again." I interpreted that as a threat of severe bodily harm if I were to find myself in such trouble again. It is hard to understand in retrospect why I harbored such fears, since Father was not a severe person. The discipline he administered was overwhelmingly verbal and based on his unquestioned position as head of the family.

Maybe Sister Phillipa just liked talking to Father, but she nailed me again just a few weeks later for some equally ridiculous transgression. If her teaching had been more captivating, perhaps I might not have been so easily distracted. I was terrified of what would happen when I told Father he had to meet again with the she bear. So, I did the only thing I could think of. I ran away from home.

The fourth-grade mind is hard to fathom. It is difficult to make any sense of what I did or what I thought I was doing as I set out on my bike with my bow and arrows to make my way in the world. I guess I thought I would live off the land. About that time I think I was reading about Robin Hood, Kipling's *The Jungle Book*, and Mark Twain's *Huckleberry Finn*. I don't think I took any provisions because I remember getting very hungry as dinner time approached. I began to see about then that this adventure had not been well planned—and might not have been a good idea at all. But I was still too scared to go home. Things would be doubly bad for me now that my disappearance undoubtedly had been discovered. Sister Phillipa would be the death of me.

So, where did I go with my bike and weapon? I'm not sure, but I know that I wound up late that afternoon in the woods along the Laurel Line tracks. I don't think there was anywhere else to go. Surely I did not expect to find game there. I was very familiar with that area and knew it provided nothing but cover.

It was March and it began to get dark about dinner time. I am not certain it was March 17, but it was close to that date because my escapade totally ruined Father and Mother's planned evening out with the O'Horas in celebration of St. Patrick's Day.

So, I was plenty hungry and cold when I encountered Kenny Bercham. Kenny and his brother John were fellow pupils at Nativity. Kenny was in Edward and Ellen's class and John was in my class, though he was a little older, having been "held back," as they used to say, for unacceptably poor academic performance. They may have been our classmates, but we did not move in the same circles. In fact, they did not move in any circles I knew of except their own. They came from a poor family that lived near the Laurel Line tracks in what can only be described as marginal quarters.

The nuns, who wore wedding rings to signify their marriage to Jesus, made life difficult for the Bercham children because they were often among the missing at Sunday Mass. Their parents apparently saw no need to force them to attend. What sin could be worse? So, the Berchams paid the price of being ridiculed, ostracized and marginalized from the rest of us. I recall having the impression that their personal hygiene was not exemplary, but that may have been erroneous. They wore clothes that were shabby and rumpled, contributing to the suspicion. In short, they were just the kind of folks that Jesus chose to consort with.

I am sure I had not been particularly nice to Kenny or his brother in the years I had known them. But Kenny did not ignore me in my time of need. He brought two potatoes from home. We pulled a few stones together, made a hearth and started a fire into which we placed the potatoes. In about 20 minutes they were thoroughly charred and could be removed from the flames. No potato before or since had tasted better—plain, without salt, butter or anything. Even the carbonized potato skin tasted good.

That took care of the hunger temporarily, but it continued to get colder. I had not planned on that. Actually it seemed I had not planned anything. I remembered that there usually was a cache of cardboard boxes on the porch of the commercial building at Prospect and Orchard, site of the neighborhood A&P, which had closed. Maybe I could make a little cardboard shelter for myself and get through the night. Remember, this was before the days of homeless folks sleeping in cardboard shelters over air vents in metropolitan areas. Could it be that I invented the idea?

I encountered another unanticipated setback when I rode my bike to that corner and found to my chagrin that there were no boxes. That was too much to take. I did not know what to do, so I just sat on the edge of the porch to plan my next move. Quite soon, a neighbor—I believe it was Claire Walsh, a cousin—came by and brought me home, but not before I hid my bow and arrows under the porch. One never knew when he might need a weapon. The entire neighborhood had been alerted and Mother was frantic. The evening out at the St. Patrick's Day dinner had been cancelled. The O'Horas and many of our relatives—who were plentiful in the neighborhood—were comforting our parents at home.

Everyone was calm when I walked in and I immediately was invited to go to bed, an invitation I accepted with relief. The next day I had a very gentle discussion with Father when he explained to me that I had misunderstood his comment on leaving the convent several weeks earlier. He apparently meant that he never wanted to go back there to meet with that nun because he realized what a nutcase she was. That was never said, for it would have been disrespectful to an authority figure—something Father would never do—but that is what he meant.

It's fair to say that all of us were pretty shaken up by that experience. I am not sure any good ever same of it, but I never, ever considered running away again. And when I went back to the porch to retrieve my bow and arrows they were gone. I guess it served me right, or so I thought at the time.

7

'Ring and Walk In'

Sometime after the Great Escapade we moved into grandmother's quarters at 224 Prospect and she took over our four rooms at 222. In retrospect, that seemed to mark a major change in all of our lives. Instead of four rooms, we now lived in seven, which meant Ellen got her own bedroom. Mother and Father slept in the front bedroom, which looked out on Prospect Avenue. Edward and I were in the middle bedroom and Ellen was in the back bedroom, which looked out on the back yard, the small house in the rear and the West Mountain in the distance. The lone bathroom was in the rear, adjacent to Ellen's room. There were three additional rooms on the third floor, which was partially finished and became a refuge for me in later years. Mostly it was used for storage, as was the basement—or cellar, as it was known to us at the time.

Grandmother's quarters needed a lot of work. There had been no renovation since Uncle Ed returned from the war and opened his medical offices in the two front rooms. He also had an office in Archbald, where he and Aunt Grace lived with their growing family. Evidence of the medical presence remained on the front door where the doorbell was embedded in a plaque that read: "Doctor's bell. Ring and walk in." I know that Mother did not want folks walking in on her unannounced, but the doctor's bell remained on the front door long past the day I left Scranton for good. Perhaps it was symbol for Mother of what she considered the greatest achievement by any member of her family—an achievement she wanted for both of her boys.

I say boys because it was unthinkable in those times that a girl would aspire to become a doctor. I know that not only from what I have read but from the experience of a woman classmate at Jefferson, whose application was denied on graduation from college with impeccable credentials because she would be "taking the place" of a man, who presumably represented a better investment of the state funds used to support medical schools. Several years and an advanced degree later, she was considered acceptable, as was I at an age that might have disqualified me earlier. Things do change.

I don't recall if it was before or after the move, but Father and Edward and I, with some help from time to time from Uncle Bob and Grandfather Carden, refurbished all rooms in the new quarters. Among the many things Grandfather Carden did in his life was to work for the Scranton Electric Company. As children we had always been warned to be particularly wary of electrical devices for fear of being electrocuted. In particular, we were warned to keep away from water any time we were using an electrical device. I can't recall that we ever knew anyone who had been electrocuted, but that was no reason to spare us the warnings. Thus, it was with great interest as well as trepidation that I observed my grandfather's peculiar method of testing electrical wires to see it they were "live." This was important during the remodeling project because some of the older electrical fixtures did not work and it was not clear whether they were getting power. Grandfather would remove the nonfunctioning fixture, detach the electrical wires, spit on his fingers and grasp one wire with the thumb and index finger of the left hand and the other wire in the same fingers of his right hand. He then would signal whether or not the wide was live. I was amazed. Surely, this was a superhuman power.

The major chore of the remodeling was steaming several layers of wallpaper off the walls and applying new paper or paint. It was a big project. I think we may have refinished the floors as well. What I remember clearly is that it was no fun; I was not cut out to be a craftsman. I knew that, of course, from working with Father from time to time to fix various things that went wrong in the house—leaky faucets, pipes, faulty electrical outlets or quirky appliances.

The scenario was always the same. Father would announce the project and Edward or I or both would be enlisted to help. Helping usually meant holding the flashlight while Father attempted to manipulate something in close quarters with poor visibility, using a tool not completely suitable for the task at hand. These were memorable if not pleasant experiences—indelibly implanted in my memory and readily recalled, I might add. What I remember vividly is vowing to myself that whatever I did with the rest of my life, as an adult I wanted to be in a position to have such tasks done by competent hired help.

In the new quarters we had two parlors—the "good parlor" or front room, into which we rarely were allowed to venture—and the middle parlor, the room where we gathered after the evening meal. It was the equivalent of a family room and the room where the television set was installed some years later when we became the last family in the developed world to obtain one. There was nothing worthwhile on television, Mother explained. So, I doubt any of us has substantial memories of Howdy Doody or Milton Berle. My only recollection of television in those days stems from the brief glimpses I got from the front doors of customers on my paper route, when I visited friends in their homes or when I walked past taverns—of which there was no shortage in Nativity—with open doors in the warm weather. I vaguely recall the 1952 election, when Eisenhower was nominated at a televised convention and defeated Adlai Stevenson handily. I think we watched the convention in Lucille Naughton's apartment on the second floor at 220 Prospect, since 224 had yet to enter the electronic age.

One of Mother's fondest ambitions in those days was to open the staircase leading from the middle parlor to the second floor. There was also a closed staircase leading from the dining room to the second floor. Under that staircase, mother wanted to create a "powder room." We were about to advance from the one-toilet Irish class to two-toilet Irish. The staircases met at the top just outside the children's bedrooms. Mother's vision included a wrought iron railing between the open staircase and the middle parlor. This was a project beyond the capabilities of Terrence S. and his crew of willing relatives and bumbling pre-adolescents. We needed hired help.

I doubt Scranton was bereft of competent home remodeling contractors. After all, the unemployment rate there at the time was in double figures and folks were hungry for work. I don't have any appreciation for the process, but the person selected to do the job was Patty (or was it Paddy?) Manley, a local drunk who could be seen from time to time staggering along Prospect Avenue. I presume he was the low bidder, a major consideration for Father and Mother. You can imagine the surprise we children experienced when this man whom we had all been advised to avoid on the street showed up at our front door to begin Mother's dream project. He rang the doctor's bell but did not walk in as instructed.

With Patty came lots of uncertainties, particularly about whether and when he would show up. One certainty was then when he received partial payment for his work, he would not be seen again for several days. I can remember wondering if he would ever show up again. Accordingly, the project ran long past its estimated completion date. When Patty was done, there was more steaming, papering and installing new carpet on the stairway by the amateur refurbishing crew. Mother was thrilled with the result, though I could see evidence of shoddy, uneven plastering under the wallpaper. You get what you pay for, I guess.

Our family emergence from the cramped quarters at 222 Prospect in some respects mimicked the liberation of a butterfly from a cocoon. We children were beginning to spread our wings and express our individuality—something that may have been partially suppressed in the crowded quarters next door. We had increased—though far from total—privacy, and we were getting older, more aware of the world beyond Nativity.

In the early years, the only pressures I can recall related to the conflict between our family values as set forth by Mother and Father and the values expressed in the behavior and lack of parental supervision of our classmates. I found it difficult to be "different" and presume my siblings did as well, though perhaps not to the same degree. Another thing I found difficult was the expectation that we would simply accept the values imposed on us without discussion. I clearly recall wondering why the various prohibitions were unaccompanied by explanations that made sense to me.

As we grew older and more independent, new conflicts began to emerge. In particular, I recall conflicts between Ella Mae, as she was known at the time, and our parents. Ella was obese and that was a matter of concern, particularly for Mother. I had the same problem, but the conflict surrounding my weight was less intense. Nevertheless, I remember wondering why Mother felt the need to remind me constantly that I was fat. Surely she should have understood that I knew I was fat and I knew that if I were to lose weight I would have to change my eating habits. But from my perspective she never missed an opportunity to remind me—a characteristic that remained true until the day she died. I vowed never to hector my children about their shortcomings.

I have no insight into what Ella thought about this but she must have felt even more harassed than I. One difference in the two of us is that I did my overeating openly, while Ella surreptitiously consumed candy and other high-calorie items. That may have been related to the greater economic resources (from my paper route) and relative freedom from supervision I enjoyed. It was a lot easier for me to buy candy or pizza—something we never, ever had at home—at the local corner store and consume it on the spot. Ella had less money, mobility and freedom and apparently when she had an opportunity to obtain treats stocked up. She had a habit of hiding her treasures in various places in her room. I remember Mother finding contraband under Ella's bed or sequestered in her dresser drawers or in her closet. These occasions were always accompanied by confrontations and unpleasantness. If it was unpleasant for me, imagine how Ella felt.

I heard an interview with Jane Fonda recently on National Public Radio. She talked of her memories of life at home with her brother, Peter, whom she said had multiple conflicts with their Father on behavioral issues. Her recollection: "I remember thinking, 'why can't he just go along'?" That instantly resonated with me because I can remember thinking the very same thing when these conflicts broke out in the home. I was definitely not the kind, understanding, nurturing brother, even though I had a personal understanding of craving for items of food and drink that were not on the approved list. A mystery to me was why the ultimate authority figure—Father—did not get involved in these conflicts. Why didn't he simply "make" Ella comply with expectations? Father was a wiser and more compassionate man than I appreciated at the time.

Father's authority was unquestioned. He made every decision Mother referred to him. Mother's ultimate power was the decision of when it was necessary to get Father involved. This was the structure under which he was raised; his Father had ultimate authority in their family. Father was nothing if not the ideal son. He not only respected his parents, he helped financially with the education of his siblings, particularly his sister, our Aunt Mary Tischer. That was one of the reasons he waited until his mid-30s to get married—that and the Depression.

As mentioned earlier, Father and his family were partners in the 1941 Chevy, which remained our family car until we bought a 1950 Plymouth just as the Korean War broke out and made cars scarce again. Mother resented the fact that when the Carden family went out for a ride in the Chevy, Grandmother Carden sat in the front seat and Mother had to ride in the back. I learned years later that behavior was common in Irish families, but that did not make it any easier for mother to accept. She was a modern woman, after all. Maybe that is why I have no memories of family car trips in the early days. The Plymouth changed all that. On weekends, the family frequently set out for rides through the countryside of Northeastern Pennsylvania. As we traveled along the many two-lane rural roads,

Father rarely missed an opportunity to comment on how wealthy the farmers were due to wasteful government subsidies. He thought like a Republican but voted Democratic.

Father's often-expressed dream at the time was to purchase a piece of property with a stream running through it. He wanted to dam the stream to create a small lake for fishing and on the surrounding land he wanted to grow Christmas trees. Mother was not impressed with or sympathetic toward entrepreneurial schemes. "What do you know about Christmas tree farming?" she would ask. Mother preferred the steady security of the post office, which, after all, offered an enviable pension. And since both Mother and Father were convinced that the Depression would recur—sooner rather than later—there was not to be a Christmas tree farm in our future.

8

Pull and Drag

As we grew older, there were more family activities. Visits from the Tischers on summer holidays often were occasions for family outings to state parks. Sometimes we would be joined by Uncle Bob and his family, Aunt Rosemary and their four daughters. When we were very young Uncle Bob and his family lived in the Washington, D.C. suburbs, where we visited them on infrequent occasions. It was a five-hour drive on mostly two-lane roads south through Wilkes-Barre and Hazleton to Harrisburg and then on to York, Pa., and into Washington. I was always impressed by the parks and monuments, but unable to understand why Uncle Bob and family did not know all their neighbors, as we did in Scranton.

We also visited often with the O'Horas, who were Father and Mother's best friends. Those visits always were preceded by extensive instruction from Mother that we were to refuse all offers of second helpings. Peg was a very good cook, so it pained me to turn down food that I craved. Peg was also very insistent, as a good hostess tended to be, so it was doubly frustrating. Mother may have thought that if we had second helpings it would imply that what we were getting at home left something to be desired.

There was always plenty of food in our house, but there was little if any effort to provide a varied or exciting menu. Father ate because he had to and did not want to experiment. In later years, when I would ask why we never had veal or some other "exotic" food that I had discovered, Mother would explain, "Your Father doesn't like veal." Had I known that he had been content to have lunches of peanut butter and jelly sandwiches daily for months, I might have understood. As it was, Father would be content with meat (meaning roast beef cooked just this side of charred through) and potatoes every evening.

Edward likes to tell a story of when he traveled to Boston on a high school trip and the group went to a Chinese restaurant. He had no idea what to order because they did not offer meat and potatoes. I can't recall a similar experience, but I do remember that in our house our idea of pasta was Chef Boyardee spaghetti from a can. We did experience meat other than roast beef. From time to time, Mother served fried beef liver (with potatoes of some kind). I think we had hamburgers and hot dogs occasionally, but I remember clearly that lunch meat was proscribed. "Not good for you," Mother explained. All of our classmates ate sandwiches with lunch meat, but not the Carden children.

Then there was the dreaded Friday menu. Friday was a day of abstinence from meat for Catholics in those days. I suppose we felt it was a rule Jesus passed down from the cross, our "charism" to bear—the equivalent of celibacy for priests—to show our devotion to the one true faith. I don't know how devoted I was but I do know that I hated the fish Mother prepared every Friday. There may have been some variation, but all I remember are the horrible fish sticks, which were no better than eating breaded sawdust. Thankfully, we could slather the breaded logs with homemade tartar sauce consisting of salad dressing (mayonnaise was too expensive), ketchup and hot dog relish. It may have been revolting but at least it had some flavor.

I don't believe it was an effort to improve our Friday menu choices, but Edward and I went fishing with Father from time to time in those days. I do recall that we ate our catch, meager that it tended to be. Those expeditions consisted of driving, usually with one of Father's friends, to a nearby lake, where we rented a boat and fishing poles. The poles were of bamboo with fishing line tied to the end. Father attached a bobber and hook with a worm to the end of the line and tossed the bobber over the side. Our job was to watch and sound the alarm when the bobber began to be pulled under the surfaces. A brisk yank on the line by raising the pole was supposed to hook the scaly creature as it devoured the worm—known affectionately as a night crawler. The plan worked occasionally, but the fish got away more often than not. Odds at a craps table in Vegas were better, I think. It is easy to understand that none of us became addicted to fishing, even years later when we got real rods and reels with shiny lures and other paraphernalia.

Another activity we shared with Father was the annual spring baseball ritual. Father was very proud of his baseball mitt, as mentioned in an earlier installment. He was fond of explaining that it was "the right kind of mitt," in contrast to the more modern and complicated baseball gloves that had been developed in the years since his childhood. Every spring it was obligatory to herald the upcoming baseball season with several episodes of playing catch with Father in the driveway we shared with the Newcomb house. There was one layer of thin leather between my palm and the ball as it came crashing into the mitt. Needless to say, I did not relish these exercises, and I presume Edward felt the same. At one point, I somehow obtained a first baseman's glove, which allowed me to catch a baseball in the webbing. This made the ritual tolerable. Father scorned the new device, but, thankfully, did not forbid it.

To this day, I can't figure out the purpose of the ritual. I don't remember any organized baseball league in which we could participate. There were occasional neighborhood pickup games played in the open space behind the textile factory next to the house in the rear of our lot. Bordering that open space along Orchard Street was a series of run-down rental quarters known to us as the "mud row." The space was limited, but we set out bases and tried to hit the ball without putting it through a neighbor's window. We were not always successful, which is why there were few opportunities to play baseball.

The "mud row" eventually was sold and demolished to make way for a new U.S. Postal Service parcel facility, where I worked during several Christmas holiday seasons while in college. Also gone was the textile plant that had been on the other side of the alley at the back of our lot. During the war the plant ran three shifts, seven days a week, but business fell off when hostilities ended. I think they made cloth for parachutes, for which there was limited demand in a peacetime economy. It should not have been a surprise that one weekend when the plant was closed fire mysteriously leveled the building. I can still remember the flames reaching skyward and burning part of the small house in the rear that belonged to Grandmother McGuire.

The plant property and the "mud row" were replaced with a gleaming new brick parcel post terminal with 18-wheelers coming and going at all hours of the day and night. Some folks might have objected to the noise, but most of the neighborhood felt it was an improvement. The fire also led to a restoration and addition to the house in the rear, where the tenants, the Sheridans, had a growing family and needed additional space.

The Sheridan children were also our age. Patsy was the oldest and I believe she was a year behind me in school. While we were contemporaries, we did not associate with them very much. I don't know why, but it could have been sensitivity by Mother to the potential for conflict with a tenant of Nellie's.

What I remember most about the Sheridans is that Mr. Sheridan was a Navy veteran of World War II and when he returned from the Pacific the best job he could get was that of a city garbage man. And to get that job he had to have political "pull"—also known at the time as "drag." Jobs of any kind were very scarce. The work was singularly unappealing, but he kept the same job for years. If he was frustrated, he apparently handled it privately.

It is hard for people today or those who grew up in other communities to understand the pernicious effect of the poor economic climate in Scranton. When I did my master's thesis at Columbia I chose the terrible economic conditions in Scranton as my topic. The unemployment rate at that time was 13 percent, but even that shocking figure did not tell the tale. There were thousands of potentially employable men and women who had stopped looking for work after years of disappointment. Who knows the true rate of unemployment at the time and for many years previously?

The local department stores offered charge accounts with payment within 120 days considered the same as cash. As mentioned earlier, neighborhood grocery stores offered credit, which allowed them to compete with the national chains. The truth is that Scranton never really emerged from the Depression, and most folks there expected disastrous times to recur. Banks were places to keep money, not to obtain loans—unless, of course, you did not need one. Wages of $100 a week were virtually unheard of and if that was your salary you were in a privileged economic class. There were no food stamps in those days, as far as I can recall, but the government did distribute "surplus food" to qualified families that applied. Many qualified but did not apply. They might have been poor but they were proud.

Growing up in that environment affected us, even though Father was never out of work. One could not avoid noticing how the Sheridan family and many others struggled. I never feared we would wind up destitute, but one never knew what the future would bring. It has been suggested that Mother instilled in all of her children a sense of competition and that competition affected their relationships with each other. After much thought, I have to say I don't believe that is the case.

If we were competing against anything, it was the hard, cruel world. We knew we had to strive to hold it at bay, to perform well enough to finish college and get a good job, preferably one with a good pension. I certainly did not want to have to rely on political connections to get a marginal job, particularly since as far as I knew we had no political connections to speak of. That work ethic set us apart from most of our classmates and we paid a price for it. In the end, I presume we would agree it was worth it.

9

Early Career Thoughts

We all knew that Father had unrequited dreams of entrepreneurship, but I did not know until after he was gone that he once came very close to fulfillment of those dreams. While Father was exempt from service in World War II, Uncle Bob, his brother, finished the University of Scranton and went into the Navy toward the end of the war. He was fortunate to be sent to electronics school and returned to Scranton with knowledge of this exotic new field.

I have no idea whose idea it was but Father and Uncle Bob decided to open a school to teach electronics to returning veterans who were eligible for GI Bill benefits. They apparently rented space and began setting up the curriculum and applied for approval to participate in the GI Bill program. Father had been trained as a teacher, so he probably felt those skills would come in handy. So what happened?

As it turns out, they did not get cold feet—a development that stops many entrepreneurial ventures before they get off the ground. The problem was that the politicians in Scranton demanded payoffs to process the application. One thing about Father: he never broke the rules and he believed no one else should, either. He was not about to pay off anyone. I can say with complete conviction that he was the most principled man I have ever known. So, there was no electronics school in our future either.

I don't know if Father planned to leave the post office, but whatever his dreams he spent his entire career of 42 years there. If he was dissatisfied with the work one would never know it. Bill Connolly, a high school and college friend who went on to a career at The New York Times, told me recently that his father "absolutely hated the post office and retired the first chance he got." Father, however he felt, continued to work long past the time he could have retired.

In his later years, I know he was dissatisfied but until then he always left for work with a smile on his face, tipping his hat to all the women he met on the street. I think his dissatisfaction toward the end of his career was based on regret that he had not sought positions that might have been available to him. On the other hand, Mother was completely satisfied with his position as head of the South Scranton finance station, a branch post office. She was happy that his position was secure and feared that had he competed for higher positions at the main post office he might get chewed up in the bureaucratic grinder. Mother always tempered ambition with caution. The shadow of the Depression was never far from her mind.

As we matured, we often heard Father talking about his entrepreneurial dreams. But they apparently did not extend to preparing his offspring for futures in entrepreneurship. Mother was right, of course; he did not know anything about running a business. Other than great-grandmother Carden who ran the speakeasy under her front porch, I know of no one in our family on either side who was in what we considered business. John and Gert Adams were pharmacists, of course, and ran a very profitable drug store. Uncle Ed McGuire was a radiologist with a private office requiring a heavy capital investment. We considered them professionals, not entrepreneurs, a word we probably had never encountered. When we talked with our parents and relatives, the only options we ever discussed were employment with good, solid corporations or the medical profession. We interacted all the time with retail merchants and others in entrepreneurial ventures, but for some reason they were not considered role models. And of the professions, only medicine was held out to be desirable, even though there were many very successful lawyers in Scranton.

Teaching was considered a worthy profession, but not ideal for boys, who, it was felt, could "do better." My recollection is that teaching was always presumed to be the career path for Ellen but I have no recollection of extensive discussions of her options. Though Aunt Gert was a pharmacist, my recollection is that pharmacy was not high on the list for consideration. Uncle Glen Tischer was an executive with Shell Oil Co. in New York and when he was in town we talked at great length about the path to success in the corporate world. We all agreed that the path led though success in high school and a "good" college, following which one would be eligible for what came to be known among some of my friends as "the big job out of town." There were very few big jobs in town and they were all taken or required political connections.

Engineering was the big thing in the early '50s. There was a shortage of all kinds of engineers, and the field was held out as a "sure thing," akin to Dustin Hoffman's "plastics." The local university had a pre-engineering curriculum, so if one was to be an engineer it meant a transfer to a university out of town or enrolling in such a place as a freshman. I had little or no preparation for the engineering curriculum since I had opted for some unknown reason for the "classics" curriculum at the Prep. Instead of biology and chemistry I took Greek, for which I had no talent and in which I had no interest.

There was medicine, of course, which Mother hoped and prayed both of her sons would pursue. I was not about to follow that path, primarily because she pressed so hard and held out her sainted brother as the embodiment of the ideal man. No one was going to tell me what to do with my life. Maybe that is why I opted for Greek instead of biology. Besides, I presumed that if I followed the path outlined above success would be inevitable in a field of my choosing. I could see myself as a successful sales executive, flitting around the country, entertaining clients at exciting places and making tons of money. Little did I know how inept I would be in that role. Luckily, I found out early enough to prevent a disastrous career choice.

Life was bleak for women in those days—or at least for women who had ambitions of pursuing a meaningful career. Many women went into the work force during the war, but most returned to their homes afterward, particularly in Scranton where work was scarce and men with families were felt to have a right to the first shot at a job. I presume there were some married women who worked outside the home, but I did not know any. The mothers of all of my classmates were housewives with no known ambitions to be part of the work force.

Mother was an exception. She returned to teaching when we were in the later years of elementary school. It did not seem like a big deal to me at the time, but in retrospect it apparently was. The female teachers in those days were primarily never-married young women and what were known as "maiden ladies," with a sprinkling of widows here and there. I know that Mother loved teaching, and I presume that she disliked being "just a housewife." We never really discussed this in the family because her returning to work did not seem unusual, according to my best recollection.

We all knew the story of her forced departure from the teaching profession when she got married and I think she made it clear she wanted to return at the first opportunity. Prior to that, I don't recall that Mother ever drove the family car—and know for sure she never drove the '41 Chevy. I believe she began as a substitute teacher in the Scranton School District. The game plan was to gain some current experience as a substitute and then apply for one of the coveted full-time teaching appointments. That required a return to school for some of the academic requirements that had been added in the intervening years.

Positive fallout for me from Mother's working was that I got to back the '50 Plymouth out of the narrow driveway between the houses and park it on the street in front of the house, ready for Mother to drive off to school. Even though I was several years under age, I had become proficient at driving Bobby Naughton's '37 Plymouth. The driveway did not pose a challenge for me. Mother was still a little shaky behind the wheel, so she welcomed the assistance. Sometimes I was not satisfied with simply backing the car down the driveway and parking it so I took it for a brief spin. Once I got in a scrape with a parked car, which caused a ruckus and the temporary withdrawal of my privileges. I was relieved that I had not been arrested. Scranton police at the time understood the foibles of youth and were more likely to call a miscreant's parents than press charges. My driving suspension put the burden on Father, so within a short time my morning duties were restored under threat of serious consequences if I were to take the car on another unauthorized spin. Some driving was better than no driving, so I accepted the restrictions.

Mother later was appointed to a full-time position as a teacher at Scranton's Hebrew Day School in the Hill Section east of downtown. At the time I did not know any Hebrews and I doubt she did either. She taught two grades, one in the morning and another in the afternoon. Her responsibility was the secular subjects—math, reading, history and whatever was not considered religious. The rabbis taught the children the Hebrew language, religion and culture. I wondered at the time why they would hire a *goy*—a term with which I was totally unfamiliar at the time—to teach Jewish children. Mother felt it was because someone unidentified with the culture would have more authority with the children. I can relate to that concept. When practicing emergency medicine in a predominantly

Jewish community in the 1980s and '90s, I grew a beard in the hope that it would give me rabbinical authority. It worked. Since mother could not grow a beard, her effectiveness in the Hebrew school may have derived from her differences from the parents, who tended to be permissive. Or maybe they hired her because she was willing to work for what they were willing to pay—something the Hill Section princesses would never contemplate.

Edward and I were at the Prep when Mother was working at the Hebrew school. It was convenient for us because she was able to swing by to pick us up after school and drive us home. As I recall she would pull up about 4 in the afternoon, which gave us some time to play basketball on the macadam outdoor court after class. Ellen was attending Marywood Seminary at the time, but I have no recollection of how she got there and how she got home. There may have been car pooling or perhaps she had to take public transportation. Edward and I were lucky because the Prep was within walking distance of our home, but Marywood was at the other end of town.

I don't know how long Mother worked at the Hebrew school, but eventually she completed the preparatory work for eligibility to apply for full-time teaching appointment in the city school district. I recall that there were some ups and downs as she prepared but do not remember what they were. She was appointed, however, and taught until she retired long after we had all left home. For Mother, teaching truly was a calling. She loved it, which apparently was why she craved a return to the classroom during her years of forced exile. Even after retirement, whenever she was exposed to children, she inquired about what they were learning in school.

In many ways, despite her caution and fears, Mother was a truly emancipated, modern woman. Yet at the same time, she was traditional. She never confronted Father about his unquestioned authority, but she learned to manipulate him to achieve her objectives. She also tried to manipulate us, but with less success. One thing we all knew, however, was that if we wanted to have Mother's unquestioned approval, a good report card worked every time.

10

Filling Our Time

School took up only about nine months of the year. That meant we had to find things to do for about three months at a time and place where there was a whole lot of nothin' goin' on. In those days I believe we had to have reached our 16th birthday to qualify for "working papers" that would allow us to have real jobs during the summer holiday. We had our paper routes, but they took up only a small part of the day. We spent a lot of time swimming and hiking along the Laurel Line tracks or up East Mountain to Mountain Lake and Lake Scranton, but there was still a lot of empty time.

In the evenings, we congregated with on the front porch with Father and Mother, Nellie and Aunt Tessie. Spring and fall chores included rituals of bringing outdoor furniture from storage and returning it there when it became too cold to sit out in the evening. The world passed by on Prospect Avenue, and most of the neighbors spent the summer evenings on their porches to watch the show. If you walked up and down the streets of Nativity you saw familiar forms seated in the shadows, with the bright glow of a cigarette here and there. Since you knew most everyone, you knew whom those silent forms represented—watching you and all else that passed by.

Among the regulars was the popcorn vendor with his push cart and high-pitched steam whistle. He pushed his cart down the street and waited at the corner for customers to appear. We were not regular consumers, but occasionally were allowed to buy a bag doused heavily with molten butter from an unsavory looking metal container. There were also ice cream vendors whose trucks had bells to signal their arrival in the neighborhood. My recollection is that we rarely were allowed to purchase ice cream. "Not good for you," Mother contended. And then there were regulars from the neighborhood, some heading to Bartoli's grocery at the corner of Hemlock and Prospect or the tavern just south of Orchard on Prospect. Among the latter was poor Patty Manley, who sometimes made his way along the east side of Prospect, across the street from our porch, nodding to all the neighbors as he passed by. On other occasions, he lurched from tree to tree, car to car or other form of support, obviously inebriated, acknowledging no one.

I recall one memorable event involving me and the front porch. I had just been told by Bobby Naughton the seminal fact of life—where it came from and how. It hadn't gotten dark yet, but the family had begun to gather on the porch, as had most of the neighbors on their porches. As usual, I was not content to keep this revelation to myself. I could not wait to share the remarkable news. So, I ran up the stairs to the porch and explained excitedly to everyone that I now understood that babies were made by a process called "fucking" by men and women that required the shedding of their clothes and a coupling of their private parts. I was not sure at that point what the differences in their private parts were, but from this coupling, according to Bobby, came babies. No one seemed surprised, but no one was willing to discuss it further. I also recall that no cross words were uttered, but I was admonished not to share my enlightenment with the immediate world.

As I got older, I escaped the evening ritual when I was recruited to hawk the "Blue Streak" edition of the morning paper at the corner of Moosic Street and Harrison Avenue. It was the first edition of the paper and was marked by a blue line or streak on the left-hand margin, added as the papers went on the conveyor belt at the Tribune Building on Washington Avenue. I don't remember how or why I had that opportunity but presume it had something to do with my morning paper route. I stood on that corner starting about 9 o'clock and held copies of the paper aloft, shouting whatever came to mind. That was how it was done in the movies, after all. Folks in their cars with the windows down—car air conditioning had yet to be developed—occasionally responded to my hawking and bought a paper. If I was lucky I got a tip as well. But tips were few and far between, given the economic conditions in Scranton.

After an hour or so, I would leave the corner temporarily to make the rounds of taverns north of Stafford Avenue on Moosic and River Streets. That broke up the routine and gave me some insight into "night life" in Scranton. Some of the taverns had juke boxes and young couples danced to the music. Those establishments also seemed likely to have food service as well. Others were for hard-core drinkers, primarily men, who sat at the bar drinking shots and beers. It seems to me that the hard-core drinkers had little interest in the day's news. Mother and

Father were not enthralled with my tour of the taverns every night, but I can't recall any bad experiences.

When I say every night, that included Sundays, when all taverns were supposed to be closed under Pennsylvania's "blue laws," which banned most commercial activity on Sundays and remained in effect until long after I finished college. Very few taverns really closed. To gain entrance, you knocked on the door. The curtain was pulled back and if you were a familiar face you were allowed in. This was a ritual I came to know quite well during my college years. Mother was unhappy that the tavern in the 300 block of Prospect operated quite openly on Sundays, turning off the neon signs in its windows as a concession to the "blue laws." I suppose Mother was unhappy that any taverns were allowed to operate at all in our neighborhood. On the other hand, Father explained that the "blue laws" had been enacted by misguided tee-totaling Protestants and, therefore, could be ignored in good conscience.

We knew very few Protestants in those days. There were good Protestants such as Uncle Glen Tischer and Uncle John Adams. Both of them had been married to our aunts in private ceremonies in the church rectory after having signed a solemn promise to raise any children resulting from the marriage as Catholics. Neither of them was a teetotaler. And then there were the bad "dirty APA" Protestants, whom we knew only the in abstract. There were some Protestant churches in our neighborhood, but who knew what went on behind those doors? One thing we knew for sure was that God would strike us dead if we even peeked inside. When the Protestant Rawson family moved in directly across the street, everyone feared that the neighborhood was going to hell. Kenny Rawson, who was our age, went to Whittier, the public school about a half block east of Nativity church on Orchard Street. I don't think I knew anyone else who went to Whittier at that time.

Other than railing against Bishop Hodur, I don't believe that the nuns taught us any overt prejudice, but we knew that Protestants were quite different from us. They had broken from Holy Mother, the one, true church, and had rejected the authority of the Pope as the Vicar of Christ on earth. What could be worse than that? Nothing I could think of, with the possible exception of the Bishop Hodur heresy. We were taught that mistakes had been made in the medieval church, such as the selling of indulgences, but these abuses had been corrected and the church had endured, just as it would until the end of time. The pope was the vicar of Christ on earth and worthy of our unquestioned loyalty. We also knew that Protestants represented majority power in the United States and would never accept a Catholic as president—as demonstrated by the overwhelming rejection of the Al Smith candidacy in 1928. We were a minority, a minority with long memories, and had to stick together to avoid being victimized. That minority stigma remained ingrained in our subconscious until the election of John F. Kennedy as president in 1960. At last, we were full-fledged Americans. The church would never be the same.

To their credit, the nuns did teach us that even Protestants could be saved and that Father Feeney from Boston had been excommunicated for teaching otherwise. I have since learned that other Catholic children in other communities were taught there was no salvation outside the church. In retrospect, the nuns did a pretty good job in insulating us from the rabid prejudice I witnessed years later in both the Catholic and public schools in Philadelphia. Of course, they were not really challenged in that regard. We had no people of color in Nativity and very few children other than those of Irish or German descent. Our Lebanese classmate, Jemella Abdella, was decidedly different, but she did not appear to suffer for it. Ralph Falzetti, on the other hand, had a difficult time with a few of the bullies in my class. Had he been a girl, they may have left him alone. That may have been the only advantage of being a girl in that neighborhood at that time.

11

The Moosic Street Hill

The corner of Moosic and Harrison, where I hawked the "Blue Streak" on summer evenings was the confluence of two major arteries. Harrison Avenue linked Nativity to the Hill Section. The Harrison Avenue Bridge over Roaring Brook gorge was a large concrete structure from which, from time to time, someone leaped to his or her death. The conventional route to Nay Aug Park crossed the bridge and turned east at the first opportunity. It was a structure with which we were very familiar, both from above and below, where Roaring Brook ran and the Laurel Line and DL (Delaware-Lackawanna) tracks lay. Harrison Avenue was also the most efficient route from Nativity to Dunmore, so it had a fair amount of traffic by the standards of the day.

Moosic Street was an even more important thoroughfare. From Nativity, if one wanted to travel to New York you drove east, up the Moosic Street Hill and on to Stroudsburg and the Delaware Water Gap. From there you crossed New Jersey, a flat expanse of small towns and tawdry neon-lit highway attractions along Route 46 designed to separate tourists from their cash. It was also the most direct route to Daleville, where Aunt Winnie and Uncle Jim had a farm. We children often went there with Father to pick huckleberries. After filling our pails, I remember sitting in their parlor and thinking it had a strange, musty aroma, a byproduct of the farm environment, I suppose. Daleville had a small airport where I saw a Piper Cub take off and land, my first close-up experience with general aviation.

Going up the Moosic Street Hill was one thing; coming down was another. There was a three-and-a-half-mile hill from top to bottom, where it leveled off for a few blocks and then plunged again at Harrison Avenue, finally leveling off for good just east of Prospect Avenue near Bob Brier's Sunoco gas station where I worked the overnight shift the summer before my senior year in high school. Moosic Street then proceeded west for about a block and a half, where it terminated at the Spruce Street Bridge. At the bridge one had the option of taking a hard right turn to cross the Roaring Brook gorge to downtown or continuing straight on Pittston Avenue, which originated at the bridge. At the Nativity end of the bridge, Harrison's Cleaners and Tailors stood on the south side and a gas station on the north. The gas station had been built on solid ground, but Harrison's had been built hanging out over the gorge, supported by steel stilts.

Jimmy Harrison, one of my classmates, was the son of an owner of Harrison's Cleaners and Tailors, which was operated by the three Harrison brothers. Jimmy's father worked fulltime for the Lackawanna Railroad, but he maintained his interest in the family business. I think both uncles worked exclusively in the tailor shop, which was a high-class operation, or at least that was my impression as a child. It seemed that Jimmy's father was rewarded with merchandise for whatever efforts he expended in support of the business; he was always sartorially resplendent. In those days I did not know Jimmy too well since he lived at South Irving and Webster, outside the boundaries of my territory. I was to get to know him quite well in later years.

Near the top of the Moosic Street Hill was a turnoff and viewing area called "the Lookout." From there you could look out over the Lackawanna Valley. At night, the city lights made the view spectacular. It is amazing how great the place looked from afar. It was also a favorite spot, I learned in later years, for young lovers to pull off and neck. On our family auto excursions through the rural countryside, we stopped often at the Lookout on the way home, so we were quite familiar with the hill. It did not seem to us at the time to pose any sort of problem. That was soon to change.

Prior to World War II, most freight in America moved by rail. I can still remember stopping with the family at the Lackawanna Station to watch the steam locomotives pull out toward Hoboken, the terminal across the Hudson from New York. They were impressive machines. It was exciting to hear and feel the power of the locomotives as they worked to pull the train forward from a full stop. The engine chugged and the huge pistons strained to move the steel wheels, which initially spun on the tracks until the train started to lurch forward ever so slightly. Then it began to pick up momentum and the wheels got a full grip on the rails. The tempo of the chugging increased until we could no longer hear the locomotive as it entered the tunnel just west of Nay Aug. As we sat in the car with the windows down, watching and listening, Mother never failed to remind us that our grandfather had been an engineer on a Lackawanna locomotive. Later came the diesels, which were hardly romantic—just large internal combustion engines mounted on wheels. Later also came the big freight trucks, which took advantage of the expanding interstate highway system begun during the Eisenhower administration. I can't recall if they had 18 wheels in those days, but they were quite large. Soon much of the nation's freight was moving by truck.

One early morning, a large truck loaded with sugar ran away on the Moosic Street Hill and crashed over the wall at the Nativity entrance to the Spruce Street Bridge, carrying Harrison's Cleaners and Tailors into the gorge. At least one of Jimmy's uncles was killed, along with the driver, I believe. And there was sugar everywhere. It was both a great tragedy and a big mess. Harrison's would never be revived as it once was. A cousin of my classmate Jimmy—also Jimmy—a glad-hander with political connections, opened a successor business, Harrison's Cleaners, in our neighborhood just across the street from Bartoli's at Hemlock and Prospect. It never became the class operation that the original was. There was always a group of neighborhood lads hanging out there. Jimmy the cleaner had political connections and ambitions but as I recall he never was successful in running for office.

That crash was the stimulus for preventive measures and the institution of hefty fines for trucks that descended the hill in an unsafe manner. Large signs erected at the top of the hill advised all trucks to stop and test their brakes before proceeding. Then, they were required to proceed in their lowest gear to the bottom of the hill. It made for a lot of slow traffic on what was essentially a three-lane highway. But folks did not want a repeat of the sugar truck crash.

There continued to be runaways from time to time, but most resulted in no serious damage. The low-gear requirement undoubtedly was working. It worked until the incident memorialized in Harry Chapin's song, "30,000 pounds of Bananas." True to the song, a truck laden with bananas careened down the hill past the level area east of Harrison and then down the second hill to South Irving where it crashed—into Jimmy Harrison's house. How much misfortune could one family sustain from one hill? I believe I was in high school at the time and was much closer to Jimmy, one of four boys from Nativity who were in my class at the Prep. My recollection is that the family moved out of the house for a time but returned when it was refurbished. Scrantonians, particularly those from Nativity, were not about to be intimidated by a little adversity.

Moosic Street was our route out of Scranton for summer vacations in Atlantic City, N.J. I don't remember much about the driving experience, except the desolation of the Pine Barrens in South Jersey, which we had to traverse to reach the beach resort. We had no appreciation for the other nice beach resorts in South Jersey because Atlantic City was the "big enchilada." As far as I know, no other resort community was ever considered. There were big hotels along the Boardwalk, which followed the beach, and hundred of smaller hotels and guest houses inland from the beach but within walking distance. We stayed in one of those—a three-story walk-up hotel with a breakfast and lunch bar on the first floor. These trips included the five of us and Grandmother McGuire. I can't recall whether we had two or three rooms, but I suspect we boys slept together and Ellen slept with grandma. In some respects, we must have resembled the Beverly Hillbillies as we unloaded the car and carried our stuff up to the rooms. Mother always had a hot plate and groceries so she could prepare breakfast for us. Eating in the hotel lunch room was a waste of money, she explained.

On our first trip I was introduced to the concept of a shared bathroom at the end of the hall. Some hotels in those days advertised "modern facilities." This was not one of them, but at least the facilities were indoors. At home we shared a bathroom, but when you emerged the person waiting to use the facility was someone you knew quite well. That was not always true in the hotel, and you had to remove your personal towels and toiletries after each use, something you did not do at home. This provided some preparation for my Army experience years later.

There was a routine to life at the shore. In the early morning, there was a brief walk along the Boardwalk. Then we changed into swimsuits and made our way to the beach. Romping in the waves was great fun, but Mother constantly cautioned us to beware of the undertow. I think we usually had lunch at the local Woolworths and returned to the beach for more romping in the waves and sunbathing. We then headed back to the hotel to change clothes and set out for supper in one of the many restaurants along Atlantic Avenue and its side streets. This was a part of the vacation I did not enjoy.

Before deciding on a restaurant, we trudged along, checking out the posted menus, particularly the prices, before deciding which establishment was worthy of our business that evening. It seemed to me to be a horrendous waste of energy, and it delayed my gustatory fulfillment, something I took seriously then as now.

And, as I recall, there was little difference in the small number of restaurants that were deemed acceptable. One thing I remember well is that Father often ordered scallops, which I found enjoyable as well. It never occurred to me to ask why we never had scallops at home. They most assuredly would have been an improvement on our usual Friday evening fare.

After supper, there was time for leisurely strolling along the Boardwalk. Highlights of the Boardwalk included the salt water taffy shops and the entertainment piers, primarily the famous Steel Pier, where as part of the entertainment viewed from bleachers erected at the end of the pier a man road a horse off a diving platform into the ocean about 100 feet below. I can't recall how the man and horse were retrieved. Visits to the piers were virtually all-day events, so were one-time events most years. The structures jutting several hundred feet over the ocean were crammed with carnival rides and all sorts of honky-tonk vendors of enticements designed to separate you from your money. There were also several movie theaters. The piers were predecessors of Disneyland, which is much more high class.

Another Boardwalk attraction was the various demonstrations of wondrous contraptions designed to make life easier—food slicing devices, cooking utensils and other items the likes of which currently are advertised on television infomercials. In those days they were demonstrated in Boardwalk storefronts by fast talking hawkers before live audiences. I must have spent hours marveling at the wonders these gadgets could perform. Very occasionally I could persuade mother to purchase one, but learned once again that Mother was right. Every device we bought on the Boardwalk inevitably proved a disappointment in the kitchen. At the far end of the Boardwalk was the famous Atlantic City Convention Center, where the Miss America Pageant was held each year. It seemed to be a special place, but I don't know why since we never got to go inside.

One could spend only so much time strolling. Even young legs get tired after awhile. Some folks rode bicycles in the evenings and early morning. Others hired pushcarts with wicker cabs, which were available for hire at all hours. We did neither. Mother thought it would have been a waste of money. When we had had enough strolling we sought refuge in one of the many covered sitting areas built on the ocean side of the Boardwalk and fitted with park benches. I can remember sitting there, watching the strollers and rich folks being pushed along the Boardwalk. A favorite pastime was to persuade grandma to "rub" our backs. "Rubbing" actually consisted of light stroking, which helped to distract us from the discomfort of the day's sunburn. Sometimes we "rubbed" each other's backs, but preferred to get that service from grandma since she had no expectations of reciprocation.

The Atlantic City vacation was an annual ritual, a ritual I tired of as I got older. Once I started working in high school I had an excuse to opt out, which I did. The only exciting thing I can remember of my brief freedom from parental supervision is that I brought home a 25-pound package of frozen shrimp from the grocery store where I was working. Shrimp was among the things we were not served at home, but I had encountered them in a shrimp cocktail somewhere. Frank Jordan, my best friend from the Prep at the time, joined me in cooking and eating all 25 pounds of shrimp. As I recall the kitchen was a mess afterward and stank to the high heaven. It's a wonder that I still eat shrimp.

12

Pubescent Sexual Curiosity

Other than my introduction to the concepts of reproduction by Bobby Naughton, I can't remember any formal or informal sex education in the early years. Nevertheless, the nuns seemed convinced that we were obsessed with sex. Why else would they be obsessed with keeping our hands out of our pockets? Whatever they did—or didn't—teach us about the physiology of reproduction, somehow they communicated the principle that any pleasure emanating from our pudendal regions in and of itself constituted a mortal sin, for which we could burn in the eternal fires of hell.

"Bless me Father, for I have sinned…" Oh, how I dreaded the weekly visit to the confessional—known colloquially as the "box"—where we presumably unburdened ourselves of unspeakable sins, particularly the reprehensible sins of the flesh. It never occurred to me as I recited the traditionally requisite five Our Fathers and five Hail Marys, my penance for my iniquities, that hearing the confessions of late prepubescents must have been the least exciting duty for a parish priest. Week after week, he had to endure a steady stream of innocents convinced that they were terrible sinners. It reminds me of those doctors who specialize in the treatment of the worried well. Since we had no known pedophiles among the many good men we encountered as children, I can't imagine that any of them enjoyed that part of the job.

I don't mean to imply that pudendal curiosity was excluded from our lives. I can recall seeing what were known as "hot books" from time to time. These were cheap comic books with pornographic themes. I don't know where they came from but they showed up occasionally and all the boys gathered 'round to view the salacious material. There were no slick magazines like *Playboy* available in those days, so we saw no pictures of real women in various stages of undress. Remember, when *Playboy* hit the newsstands it was kept under the counter and mailed to subscribers in a plain brown wrapper. The government tried unsuccessfully to shut it down. In the absence of authentic material, we had to rely on our imagination, aided and abetted by the occasional "hot book."

Somehow the girls we knew in school seemed a different species from the images encountered in the "hot books." Our exposure to real young ladies likely to stimulate prepubescent sexual curiosity was limited. Among these were our next-door neighbors, Claire Walsh and Bobby Naughton's sisters, Jeannie and Joannie. All three were cousins and seemed much older at the time. Jeannie was in high school. She had been among the first class to graduate from Nativity School. I clearly remember watching Jeannie paint her legs before going out on a date. Nylons simply were unavailable during the war, so young women painted their legs to simulate stockings. At the time I was sure that Jeannie was one of the most beautiful women in the world.

About the seventh grade, curiosity was supplanted by strange feelings of what was condemned by the nuns as "carnal desire," stimulated internally by raging hormones and externally by the budding breasts of our female classmates. We began to view these classmates differently. Up to that point they had been an inconvenience, the weaker sex favored by the nuns because they were better behaved than the boys and more likely to display more diligence in completing academic assignments satisfactorily. It was in seventh grade that we began to understand that they might be of interest to us after all.

Parochial schools in the Scranton Diocese were coeducational, something that I learned later was not true of many other dioceses where there were schools for boys and schools for girls. That gave us plenty of opportunity to observe as these young women who consecrated themselves to the Blessed Virgin each May began to fill out the dark green jumpers of their school uniforms. This process was a matter of fascination for the boys, who also dedicated themselves to the Virgin every May. It was all about virginity, stupid! And if there is one thing I know for certain, we were all virgins, and destined to remain so for a long time.

But one could always hope and dream and, of course, gossip. The girls were experiencing parallel changes based on their bodily maturation and internal hormones. They suddenly began to take much more care with their appearance. They preened while the males strutted. At the Globe Theater Saturday matinee they paraded endlessly up and down the aisles, back and forth from the lobby.

No human has to use the rest room that often. Gossip centered on the more viva-cious and comely young ladies, those most popular with the largest number of boys. The girls who developed more slowly or who exhibited more introverted social tendencies were not subjects of speculation, all of which, of course, was pure fantasy.

About seventh grade, we began to partake in a Nativity social custom that I have not encountered anywhere else. Various classmates began hosting parties to which an equal number of boys and girls were invited. I don't recall the prelimi-naries or the details of parental supervision, if any. But the real business of the party was the "making out" experience. We all sat around the living room of the host home and paired off. There was a process for switching partners, but I don't remember those details either. The lights were turned down and the pairs began by hugging and kissing tentatively, what was known at the time as "necking." As we became comfortable we might progress to the sinful "French kiss," which for some reason was not known as "tonguing" and some of the girls would refuse to allow. Eventually it became known among the boys who was "easy" and, there-fore, a more desirable partner. Interestingly one of the girls who provided the most passionate kissing entered the convent directly after high school. It is, per-haps, unique to Nativity in the early 1950s that the boys and girls learned the art of kissing before they learned to dance. But we all know what dancing can lead to.

Needless to say, I was not among the hosts for such goings on. Mother and Father would never allow it. I'm not sure why other parents did, but these parties were not rare occurrences. What I do recall from those days is that I fell in love with Janeann Nealon, a slight brunette, who I believe had recently moved to Nativity. Perhaps it was her newness that attracted me, because I don't believe she stood out for her physical development or social graces. At any rate, the attraction was not mutual and she broke my heart. She paired off with Billy O'Boyle, a cousin of our Aunt Rosemary, who became captain of the basketball team at South Catholic High School. When Janeann showed up at Father's wake it was the first time I had seen her in more than 30 years. She was still married to Billy.

I was destined to leave this group of classmates and the innocent mutual explora-tion of our sexuality. I and three other boys from Nativity matriculated at Scran-ton Prep, where the student body was much more diverse in one respect, but excluded girls. Catholic girls whose parents had aspirations for their daughters' education and social standing, sent their girls to Marywood Seminary, the high school affiliated with Marywood College, which counted Mother among its alumnae. Ellen also became one of those known by the Prep boys as the Marywood girls, two populations destined for each other. In retrospect, it is amazing how quickly the ties built up over eight years of coeducational experience at Nativity dissolved and new ties developed with the unisex Marywood community.

When I entered the Prep I believe I knew only one of the Marywood girls, Pat Lawless, who happened to be born the same day as I at the Mary Keller Hospital at the top of the Hickory Street Hill. Pat had been a classmate at Nativity for the first four years, when her family moved from Moosic Street to Green Ridge, just a few blocks from Marywood. I don't believe I knew at the time that she had enrolled at Marywood instead of the parish school, St. Paul's. In fact, I don't believe that Marywood had even entered my consciousness at that point. There were too many new things to get used to at the Prep.

One day, Frank McDonnell, a classmate from the Hill Section, inquired whether I was interested in attending the first formal dance of the year at Marywood. I'm not sure I even knew how to dance at that point. Knowing how to kiss didn't count. But I was nothing if not game for anything new, so I agreed. I was instructed to await a phone call from one of the young ladies. That was how it was done. A day or so later, Irene Sexton called and invited me to the dance, a semi-formal affair where I was required to wear a suit. She wore a gown adorned with a flower of some sort provided by me (selected and purchased by Mother). I was beginning a whole new experience. But at that age I needed Mother to provide transportation. She drove us to the dance at the Marywood campus and picked us up afterward at Preno's, the downtown restaurant where we all went by cab after the dance and where I had my first encounter with pasta that did not come out of a can. The front parlor make-out parties were much less complicated.

To reciprocate for invitations to the formal dances at Marywood, there were counterpart events sponsored by the Prep, to which we invariably invited the same Marywood girls who invited us to their dances. It was a closed circle, and most of the parents would not have had it any other way. After all, they considered their children the elite of Scranton and it was only proper that they should mingle and, perhaps, map out future lives together.

Other than the dances at our high schools, there was some opportunity to meet young ladies who moved in other circles. I was particularly lucky in that regard in that South Catholic sponsored square dances every Monday night in the Nativity School auditorium. Square dancing apparently was considered "safe" by the nuns since direct contact with your partner was limited and mostly side-to-side instead of frontal, which was too characteristic of the missionary position to be allowed. Boys and girls stood around in separate clusters with the boys peeling off one by one to ask a young lady to honor him with a dance. I attended these functions often even though Monday was a school night and my primary duty presumably was to spend at least three hours on my homework. Trivial pursuits like dancing were no excuse for skipping your homework. Only truly important conflicts like basketball games were acceptable. Square dancing was fun, but I don't remember meeting anyone new with whom I considered having a more long-term relationship.

I doubt many of us were thinking about lives of married bliss at that stage, but I am sure most of us thought a lot about sex, about which we knew very little but about which we craved to know a lot, especially through direct experience. One thing we knew about the Marywood girls was that they were not eligible targets for the big score. In fact, none of the good Catholic girls we knew were eligible as long as they remained under the watchful eyes of the nuns. But there were young ladies who attended the various public schools around town whose morality was automatically suspect. After all, if they valued chastity, why did they opt out of the Catholic school system?

One of these girls was from a Catholic family in Nativity who chose to enroll at Scranton's Central High School. Mother and Father were graduates of Central but they attended prior to the availability of a Catholic high school education. It was immediately surmised by the neighborhood adolescent males that this young lady lusted for sex, just as they lusted for sex. There was no appreciation of differences in male and female sexuality. If a girl was free of domination by the nuns why would she not crave carnal pleasure? It is clear that our education in sexuality and reproductive physiology was sorely deficient.

And despite all the fantasies and gossip, I don't think anyone I knew was sexually active. For one thing, we had little knowledge of contraception and less access. Those were the days before the pill and if one found a willing partner and wanted to reliably avoid unexpected parenthood, the "rubber" was your only recourse. "Rubbers," or prophylactics, "sold for the prevention of disease only," were available from only two sources. The first was the neighborhood drug store where no self-respecting Catholic adolescent would have the temerity to ask the druggist to bring the desired implement from behind the counter, where they were kept. I am sure most of us felt the druggist was likely to meet such a request with a phone call to our parents. The second was the grimy dispensing machines found in the rest rooms of some gasoline stations. There were too many apocryphal tales of "rubbers" with pinholes intentionally placed for us to trust any product dispensed in a rest room. Besides, carrying a packet of "rubbers" around in one's wallet addressed only half of the challenge. Finding a willing partner was virtually an insurmountable obstacle in Scranton of the 1950s. Despite all the gossip about "loose" young ladies, I can't remember a single "shotgun wedding" during our high school days.

13

Celebrating Diversity

While I was unfamiliar with the Marywood crowd when I entered the Prep, it is a sure bet that Father and Mother were familiar with their parents, in particular the parents of the girls of Irish descent who made up the group with which my friends at the Prep socialized. That is not to suggest that the Prep experience mirrored the Nativity neighborhood, where nearly everyone was of Irish or German descent. Prep was a true melting pot for a wide variety of ethnicities representing successive waves of immigration from Europe to Northeastern Pennsylvania.

The Irish came to escape the potato famine in the mid-1800s, followed by the Italians, Polish, Lithuanians, Ukrainians, and other Eastern Europeans. All came for jobs as common laborers in the mines, which were the major industry in the Lackawanna and Wyoming Valleys. The Welsh, who were skilled miners in their own country, came to supervise the rest of the miners, earning for themselves the everlasting enmity of the immigrant community. Sainted Grandmother Nellie McGuire never had a bad word for anyone—except the Welsh. Never mind that they were fellow Celts.

We had escaped learning any militant or overt prejudice at home or from the nuns, but we had been sheltered in the reasonably homogeneous Nativity. At Prep we rubbed elbows with children representing all of the immigrant communities who traveled daily from as far north as Honesdale and as far south as Wilkes-Barre and Kingston. There may have been boys from south of Wilkes-Barre as well. Some of them came via the Laurel Line, which ran commuter trains between the two Northeastern Pennsylvania "metropolises." We came from very different backgrounds, but we had one thing in common—all of our parents wanted better lives for their boys and felt the Prep would give them the best chance of achieving that. As I met and befriended boys from other cultures, mother would invariably ask, "What kind of name is that?" when I mentioned a new friend. Examples of names Mother found unfamiliar were Bartechhi, Balish, Antal, Grysbicki and Kraniak. She had no trouble with Connolly, Rafferty, Harrison, Jordan or O'Brien. By that time I had developed a response. "It's an American name, Mother," I would reply. That gave me great satisfaction but did not end the inquiries.

Michael Alumni was a boy from what we called "up the line," a series of small towns stretching from Scranton north to Carbondale. All seemed to be dominated by one or another ethnic group. Michael's mother scrubbed floors so she could afford the $200 tuition bill. Tuition there now is $7,400 a year. Mrs. Alumni was not atypical; there were plenty of boys from families of limited means. Michael's mother's dedication paid off. Michael was smart. He was always on the honor roll and went on to success. I am not sure what career he chose, but I believe it was in physics or engineering. I mention him here because I see every year that he makes substantial donations to his alma mater. I'm sure he appreciates what his mother did for him.

The Jesuits were very sensitive to the disparities in backgrounds. We had barely finished our orientation to the school when they began to schedule "class days" on Saturdays. Each boy was asked to bring an item of food typical of his culture. We would then discuss the various food preparations and the cultures they represented. I have no idea what I brought since meat and potatoes isn't exactly lunch or picnic fare. On other occasions the Jesuits took small groups of students on hikes and other excursions where we came to know each other quite well. I can still remember the Reverend Mr. John Hugh Duggan, S.J., a happy Irish Philadelphian, whipping up what he called a "goplet"—a mixture of eggs and most anything else you might imagine—in a frying pan for a hungry group of hikers from very diverse backgrounds. The Jesuits taught us in a subtle way to celebrate our diversity, something for which I remain extremely grateful.

Whether it was the class days or the rigorous academic challenge, we formed a cohesive group of what some of our former friends called "Prepper pots." Other than the Marywood girls, we had few admirers among the students at the other Catholic high schools in the area. I presume they considered us elitists, which was partially true since The Scranton Prep Cavaliers were the best basketball team in the Catholic League year after year. Sometimes it is hard to be humble. We also stood out with our purple and gold Eisenhower-style jackets, under which, typically, the tails of the sports jacket that was required attire in school were tucked.

Since our student body came from nearly everywhere, these jackets made our presence felt up and down the valleys.

We had no boarding students at the Prep, but there were some at Marywood. They were the children of wealthy Catholics who wanted to stash their precious daughters in a "healthy" environment during their susceptible years so their virginity could be preserved. They could not have picked a better place, since, as we have seen, the nuns seem to obsess about virginity. I can remember a sense of liberation when the Jesuit scholastics—seminarians such as Mr. Duggan on three-year teaching assignments—began to make fun of the nun experience virtually all of us boys shared. It was clear that they all had had similar experiences and had not only survived but thrived. We were not scarred forever, after all.

The Jesuits were wonderful mentors for male adolescents as we came to grips with the challenges of the world. I will never forget an experience I had with Father John Ryan, SJ, the prefect of discipline. How many schools today have a prefect of discipline? I was in a typical adolescent state of despair about something or another—the issue is long since forgotten—and I was bending Father Ryan's ear with my tale of woe. My proposed solution: "I think I should quit school and join the Navy," knowing full well that my parents would not allow that to happen. "That's a good idea, Terrence," he responded without missing a beat. End of conversation. I had learned something: whining was not going to get me any sympathy.

We learned from the Jesuits that no topic was off limits for study or discussion. They celebrated the power of intellect to understand and deal with any problem—with their guidance, of course. To this day, I am grateful for the appreciation these men gave me for intellectual inquiry and the confidence they gave me in the power of rational analysis. Until recently, I had absolutely no misgivings about any of the values I accumulated at that high school, which I still credit for much of the success and confidence I have enjoyed in life. Recently, however, after reading the memoir of a former Jesuit seminarian, I have come to wonder about the wisdom of instilling in us a total dedication to achievement of any task we have chosen for ourselves. Sometimes that dedication distracts our attention from other pursuits that might or could have enhanced our happiness and satisfaction.

The freedom and encouragement to consider any intellectual topic led to conflict at home. Father was convinced that Edward and I were learning heresy from the Jesuits. He was a fully conventional, traditional Catholic, so traditional that he had the family participate in Father Peyton's Family Rosary Crusade. The theme of the crusade was, "The Family That Prays Together Stays Together." After a full day with the wimpled warriors, I was in no mood for another half-hour of piety and did not feel the cohesion of our family was in danger if we omitted this one ritual. By that time we had learned the value of passive resistance quite well and the evening ritual eventually was suspended in our household.

Father was uncomfortable as Edward and I under the guidance of the Jesuits began to tease out the "optional" from the essential tenets of our faith. It is best not to question anything, Father felt. What if these inquiries—horror of horrors—led to a loss of our faith? Father knew a man in his childhood who had gone on to some fancy college and lost his faith. It was clear that Father believed this was the worst tragedy that could befall any man. He told that story often. Mother did, too.

These discussions took place at the kitchen table and sometimes got loud when there were disagreements, so loud that Mother would run over and close the kitchen windows so the neighbors would not heard the discord in our house. Those were the days before home air conditioning and folks left their windows open most of the time from late spring to early fall. It was not in my nature—then or now—to back down when I thought I was right. And Father did not expect his views to be challenged. After all, he was the head of the family, the supreme authority. While I was learning the fine art of debate in school—a skill both Mother and Father applauded when I was on stage with the debate team—they would have preferred that these skills be left at the front door of the family home.

I have lived to regret those confrontations. Late in life when he was hospitalized, Father asked me to bend over his bed. He was having trouble speaking, but it was clear that he was asking me whether I loved him. I was devastated. How could he have any doubt? Winning the argument, whatever it was about, was not worth creating any doubt in his mind of my fundamental love and respect for him, a respect that has grown in the years since his death. I can relate to those who express feelings of loss for a deceased parent. I can't help but wish that I had said many things that I didn't and had not said many things that I did.

14

Conformity Cramped My Style

Recently I attended a Saturday lecture at a high school in one of the most poverty-stricken neighborhoods of Tucson. Perhaps it was the contrast between the desperate conditions in which most of the residents of that neighborhood live and the sumptuous nature of the high school facilities, but I could not help but recall the building in which I received my high school education. As mentioned earlier, Scranton Prep occupied a former private hospital at the intersection of Wyoming Avenue and Mulberry Street. Next door was the seedy Palace Hotel, about which there were constant rumors of unsavory activities between consenting adults. To the south was LaSalle Hall, in which some of our Jesuit instructors lived, and Old Main of the University of Scranton, where most of my classmates eventually matriculated.

The Prep was a bare-bones facility. There was no gymnasium. The only athletic facility was the macadam basketball court between the Prep Building and LaSalle Hall. It was busy virtually every day of the school year if not covered with snow. There was a locker room and cafeteria in the basement, along with the senior smoking room, the only place within a block of the school where a student was authorized to smoke. One had to survive the gantlet of the first three years to enter that hallowed space. It gave us something to look forward to. On the first floor was the office of the headmaster, the fire-breathing John A. Convery, SJ, who loved to remind us that if we didn't like it there we could always "get out." He knew that our parents would kill us if we took him up on the offer.

Across from the headmaster's office was the library, pretty limited by today's standards. The prefect of discipline also had an office on the first floor, and I believe there was a classroom at the north end of the building, a classroom that hosted the traditional Jesuit disciplinary ritual for miscreant students—Jug. If one were assigned to jug he had to forgo the afternoon basketball game on the macadam court and delay his departure for home until 4:30, which meant I had to walk home that afternoon. I spent a lot of time in jug.

On the second floor was the Assembly Room, where we gathered for Mass. We used the *Missa Recitata* liturgy, which was revolutionary for the time. The priest would intone a prayer and we would respond in unison and in Latin. The congregants actually participated in the liturgy, unlike the conventional Tridentine ritual during which the priests and congregation did their best to ignore each other. The rest of the building was devoted to classrooms and faculty offices.

Whenever we had classes in rooms on the west side of the building with a view of the Palace Hotel, we could not help but sneak occasional peaks to see if any of the ladies of the evening had hung out their bloomers to dry. We had vivid imaginations. Those were the days before home laundry driers so clothes were dried on rope clotheslines in the back or side yards. To my knowledge none of us ever spotted a real lady of the evening or her bloomers. We overlooked the possibility that their laundry was sent with the hotel sheets, pillow casings and towels to a commercial laundry. We also overlooked the possibility that these mysterious unseen courtesans were simply mythical figures of urban legend, since prostitution in Scranton has been cleaned up in the early days of World War II. Nevertheless, their potential presence gave us something to talk about.

Since we had no athletic facilities, our championship basketball team had to find a place to practice. John Gallagher, the coach, arranged for the team to practice at the Pennsylvania Oral School for the deaf in Green Ridge. I had volunteered to serve as "manager" of the team during my last three years at Prep. Manager actually was a euphemism for go-fer or schlepper. It also meant a trolley ride from downtown to Green Ridge two or three afternoons a week with a duffel bag full of basketballs and a trolley ride home that night after practice. Sometimes on weekends and during holiday periods we would practice at the South Scranton Junior High School gym, where the Prep played its home games. I can't help but recall those days when I visit a modern school where, despite lackluster academic performance, the students are provided facilities beyond anything we could ever dream of. That is not true, of course, in the inner cities of the older cities, but it is true in much of the nation.

Lackluster performance was not tolerated at the Prep. Some of the teachers used tactics that would most assuredly get them fired or even prosecuted today. Intimidation and ridicule were considered valid techniques for motivating students. And some of the slower students—in this case, slow is a relative term—found themselves repeated targets. No one seemed to think a thing of it. Maybe bullying from instructors was easier to take than bullying from fellow classmates, since I can't recall anyone suffering psychologically. I presume there are those who would challenge that judgment.

The academic program was intense and concentrated on the classics. Two periods of Latin were scheduled every day in the first year, along with algebra, history and composition. There were no study periods and no fluff classes. The only respite was the two classes of "health," a state requirement, each week. The curriculum was equally rigorous for all four years. In the second year, the class was split into those opting for Greek and those who were to take biology and chemistry, along with math and the social studies courses. We all took physics in our senior year. Foreign language options were French, German and Spanish. Those who took Spanish were considered less serious students. Every student was expected to spend at least three hours a night on homework, a requirement that most of us ignored during basketball season.

High school was a major rite of passage related to another life experience—employment. We became eligible for working papers at 16 and the summer after I passed that milestone I got a job in a downtown independent grocery store owned by a man named Al Bielinski. Al may have been the stingiest man I encountered in my working life. He paid me and Johnny Lafferty 50 cents an hour to stock shelves, clean up, staff the meat counter and operate the cash register at the front of the store. We were the night crew primarily, taking over in late afternoon from the regulars and serving all customers' needs until 9 PM. What we didn't know is that Al was not only penurious but he was suspicious. We learned that he often spied on us from the second floor of the Comerford Theater across the street. He wanted his full 50 cents worth for every hour we were paid.

After awhile, outwitting stingy Al became a game on which Johnny and I thrived. We loved to sneak a small bottle of chocolate milk, a package of cup cakes or other treat without paying for it. With Al possibly spying on us from the theater across the street, we learned to be discrete. Sometimes we stashed treats in the garbage bin at the back of the store, but we learned to our dismay that he even checked there. It would have been so much simpler had he opted to pay us the same as comparable workers in the two adjacent grocery stores on Wyoming Avenue.

Al also offered a delivery service to customers who could not make it to the store. He had a decrepit 1941 Plymouth coupe with a stick shift transmission and a huge trunk. The car should not have been on the road much less used as a commercial vehicle. I have nightmares sometimes recalling an experience I had in West Scranton one weekend while delivering orders in the '41 Plymouth. West Scranton backed up to West Mountain and was hilly, just like South Side. There was snow on the ground, but that was not a big deal. If you were to drive in Scranton, you had to know how to drive in snow. But as I was descending a hill the brakes locked, throwing the old heap into a spin, which in and of itself, was not alarming. But then, the driver's door flew open. This was before seat belts and there was nothing but the wheel for me to hold onto. I was thrown from the vehicle and to this day can recall the image of the rear wheel bumping over the snow as it careened toward me, lying helpless on the street. It struck me and sent me sliding across the snow-covered street out of harm's way. Such escapes in those days were attributed to one's guardian angel. I was unhurt and—wonder of wonders—the Plymouth missed all available targets of opportunity and wound up against the curb, headed back where it had come from, with the engine still running. I know that I drove the car back to the store after making all of the assigned deliveries, but I believe I refused to deliver any more orders for Al.

At the first opportunity I left Al's employment and took a job at a new A&P super market along Meadow Avenue up the Hemlock Street hill from my home. Overnight, I went from 50 cents an hour to $1.40 and had to join the Retail Clerks International Union, which was responsible for the higher wage. We had much more professional scheduling, supervision and training at the A&P, which made Al's operation look bush league. I was disappointed that I could no longer work on the meat counter, for that was a different skill under the union contract and I did not qualify. But the money was so much better and the job was much closer to home. I worked there from my senior year in high school through most of college.

The only issue I had with the A&P was that it was totally inflexible. Everyone was expected to work in the same way and at the same speed. This was never stated, but it was obvious that those who tried to adopt a work style that suited their personalities were suspect. I was one of those. I loved to work as a checker and I was very good at it. Those were the days before bar codes. We had to enter the price of every item on the cash register and the department under which it was to be charged—meat, produce, dairy, groceries. When the total was tallied, we were expected to make change and our cash drawers were expected to tally out at the end of the shift.

I was an extremely fast checker—and accurate as well, a fact of which I was confident because the store manager, John Philbin, made a habit of confirming my tallies on a regular basis. He did not like the fact that I was able to rush through the price entry process since I knew most of the prices and rarely had to consult a reference. But when I was through putting in the prices of all the items I took my time bagging the orders and chatted with the customers. That was my style. After all I knew most of the customers and they knew me and my family. This was Nativity, after all. Philbin eventually decided that I would be assigned as a checker only when absolutely necessary. From that point on, I was relegated to standing in the parking lot front of the store to help folks put their groceries in their cars or to stocking the shelves. Usually, I did not mind the parking lot assignment because I was able to chat with the customers outside the visual field of John Philbin. Actually I preferred working outside during the good weather, but there is precious little of that in Scranton. I should have known then that I would never be happy working for a corporation. Conformity cramped my style.

Since I worked at the A&P several afternoons a week as well as all day Saturday—stores were not open on Sundays because of the "blue laws"—I depended on Mother to drive me to work when she got home from school. One day, however, I found myself in a predicament, the details of the creation of which escape me. What I do recall is that I was home, the car was home and Ellen was home and Mother was not home. There was no way I could have walked up that hill and clocked in on time. Not to worry, after all we now had a new 1957 Plymouth with a push-button automatic transmission. All one had to do was put it in drive, point it in the right direction and take off. I decided Ellen would drive me to work. That she did not have a license was of little concern. After all, I had driven for years without a license. And the hardest part of learning to drive, I felt, was learning to operate the clutch in a car with a manual transmission. Since the Plymouth was an automatic, driving it was a piece of cake—or so I told myself.

I asked Ellen to get in the car with me and I drove to the work site. I don't recall if I told her what I had in mind, but she had to know. At any rate, I showed her how to operate the automatic transmission and pointed out the brake pedal and accelerator. When in doubt, hit the break, I instructed. She accepted the instruction, pulled out and drove the car home without incident. She really came through when I needed her. I wonder if I made it clear how appreciative I was.

15

'Enoof Is Enoof'

From time to time folks have asked me why I retired in September, 2000 at the age of 62. Many physicians work long past that age. I learned recently that John Ward, a physician I knew and admired in Illinois, had died at age 97. I believe he continued to see a few patients into his early 90s. So why did I quit when I did, and was it the right decision?

I suppose there are a host of reasons, but two stand out. First, I retired because I could. I have been blessed with financial security, for which I am thankful. Perhaps I should modify that statement to say it appears I have been blessed with financial security. No one from the Scranton of my youth every feels truly financially secure. After all, any day now we could have another Depression. Secondly, as a very wise old Irishman once said, "enoof is enoof." I had worked continually from the age of 10 until I retired. "Enoof **is** enoof!" Translation: it was the right decision.

As recounted earlier, I am not sure what motivated me to start working so early. I'm sure the monetary reward was a factor, but I think in looking over my entire life to date that the driving force was the opportunity to experience something new. Mother understood that I was easily bored and she worried about how this would affect my future. After all, Father worked 42 years in the post office and that suited her quite well. She understood that I was not cut out for a career doing anything for 42 years. She understood me better than I understood myself.

I mentioned how I resisted regimentation while working at the A&P. Too bad I failed to understand at point in my life the significance of my unwillingness to be molded to fit the needs of an employer. I began to understand by the time I hit 50 that I was destined never to work happily **for** anyone or any organization. On the other hand, I could be and was happy working **with** anyone or any organization. Lest anyone think this was because I was unwilling to work hard, be assured that it is infinitely more risky and difficult to be your own person than to fit into a corporate structure. Before I retired I was inducted into the Entrepreneurship Hall of Fame of the University of Illinois at Chicago. At the induction dinner, several of the more celebrated inductees spoke briefly. I was struck by how all of them related the same theme—the terror of knowing you had to meet a payroll and not sure how you were going to do it. My family is well aware that I was always the last person to be paid, yet I am the first to concede that for me it was worth it.

Father had unrequited dreams of entrepreneurship. I was destined for entrepreneurship but did not know it. If genes mean anything, I've often thought that I inherited Mother's ambition and drive and Father's brains, a great combination for what I ultimately did with my life. But as a child, as noted earlier, I believed the ideal career for me was to find a good company with opportunity for advancement and settle in until eligible for retirement. Good companies in those days were IBM, Sears, Xerox, Kodak and others known for patronizing, covenantal relationships with their employees.

But this is not a tale about my career. In some ways it is about my preparation for what became my career, beginning with those paper routes, which were touted by the publishers as a healthy introduction to sound business principles. I may have learned some sound business principles from that experience but for the moment I can't think of any other than keeping track of the cash, knowing where every dollar comes from and where it goes.

Working in grocery stores taught me that one had to show up at the appointed hour, as documented by a time clock, and produce at a level and in a manner acceptable to your supervisor. I preferred a job where the supervisor told you what to do and then let you alone to do it in your own way and at your own pace. Working the night shift at Bobby Brier's gas station was like that. I showed up at 11 P.M. and was in charge until the next morning. In charge of what, you might ask. There was no one there but me. Across the street, the Griffiths bothers, Tommy and Paul, shared the night shift in their father's Texaco station. I liked being in charge and being left alone. Mind you, I was not mechanically gifted, so folks who showed up in the middle of the night with real problems got little assistance from me. However, I could pump gas and make change, and my cash always tallied against the record sheet in the morning. And I did not fall asleep on the job. Actually, at that stage of life it was exciting for me to be awake all night.

At the A&P you were not left alone. You were not asked your opinion or for suggestions. There was a job to be done and you were to do it in the manner and time prescribed by someone else. There were no annual performance reviews during which your reaction was solicited. At the A&P, your hourly rate was determined by union negotiators you never met. I suppose I tolerated those conditions because I knew they were temporary. Someday I would graduate from college and secure the "big job out of town."

I didn't worry much about what career I ultimately would choose. As mentioned earlier, I had a vague notion that I could be a successful sales executive in a national corporation. I expected the skills in analysis and debate I had learned would help me to overcome any resistance on the part of a customer to the product I was pitching. Wow, was I naïve.

Thankfully, I got an opportunity during my first year of college to learn how nonsensical my views of a career in sales were. Jimmy Rogan, a cousin of Billy, who was a classmate at Nativity, was in my class at the university. He was somewhat older, having returned to college after a stint in the military. There were a lot of Korean War-era vets in school with us because of the GI Bill, which covered most of their expenses. Jimmy was a serious student in the business department, which those of us who had been schooled in the classics thought less serious than the liberal arts, which, of course prepared one for nothing. I can't recall how we got involved together as rookie medical insurance salesmen, but I do recall that Jimmy recruited me.

The company had a sales office in the Glen Alden Coal Co. Building near campus. We had a brief orientation during which we were introduced to a canned sales pitch that the company felt would yield the best results. Then we got to go into the field with a couple of experienced salesmen to see how it was done. I should have known that there was something wrong when I met the role models. Both of them were fairly scruffy, uneducated types who I learned later were veterans of door-to-door encyclopedia sales. I should also have done some due diligence on the product, but at that stage in life I thought any company with an office in a respectable building in town would be respectable. The sad truth is that I was so anxious to show how effective I could be in the field that I would have ignored the most flagrant warning signs imaginable. It never occurred to me that any legitimate company with a sound product would not have been about to hire an eager college student with no experience.

During my field training, I noticed that the redneck pitchmen used the canned presentation almost exclusively. They did not tailor their approach to the individual customer or even respond directly to objections or questions raised. I also noticed that instead of canvassing homes in a city neighborhood, where they could reach many more potential customers in a given period of time, they prowled the rural roads outside of town, looking for folks who lived in what they called "crap shacks." It became clear fairly quickly that they were counting on the potential customers being unsophisticated. I presume that is why the company called its products the Blue Plans, which most folks in the "crap shacks" confused with Blue Cross, probably the best known and most reputable medical insurance company at the time.

I was so anxious to demonstrate my inherent abilities that none of that made an impression initially. That quickly changed when I found that my approach was totally unproductive. Other than the opening, which got me in the door, I eschewed the canned presentation and tried to focus on the needs and questions of the potential customer. One thing I knew I could not do was to lie to them. If there is a truth gene, I inherited it from Father. That may have been my fatal flaw as an insurance salesman, since it became apparent rather quickly that I was wasting my time, so I moved on.

The experience was helpful in several respects. I never again entertained fantasies of success as a sales executive, and I had broadened my experience, something I have always valued. I was still working between 19 and 29 hours a week at the A&P, so this brief escapade had no meaningfully deleterious effect on my financial situation. One thing it did not accomplish was to bring into question my vision of the future—a career with a benevolent national corporation where I could advance through the ranks according to my considerable talents.

Among my many work experiences as a young person one stands out as particularly atypical. One summer during college we had brush fires throughout Northeastern Pennsylvania and I found myself on a crew working a fire in South Scranton near the Valley View public housing project. I have no recollection of how I got involved, but the pay was good and it broadened my experience. We attacked the fire with rakes, shovels, portable water tanks carried on our backs and Indian pumps to spray it on the flames. These implements may seem crude but they proved effective and we had the fire under control in a single day. Nevertheless, the crew chief informed us there were plenty of hot spots to worry about and it could spring up again at any time.

A decision was made that we would bivouac overnight near the fire in case there was a resurgence and would patrol the site the following day to eliminate hot spots. This just added to the excitement. I loved it. Besides, we were getting paid simply for standing by. Government work has its benefits.

During the night we noticed a car pull into an open field near the fire site and turn off its lights. We suspected why the driver had selected this location and that he was totally unaware that 30-40 young men were camped out a hundred yards to his south. After about 15 minutes the group could not longer contain itself. A delegation was formed to inform the unwary driver that he was parked in a fire zone and had needlessly endangered himself and his presumed passenger.

The delegation approached the car from the front and on cue shone their flashlights on the unsuspecting couple, both "nekked" as jaybirds *in flagrante delicto*. This, too, added to my experience and convinced me that the back seat of a car parked in a darkened field was not a reasonable place to pursue a sexual liaison. Needless to say, the driver and his embarrassed passenger wasted no time in exiting the fire scene.

A work experience that contributed practical knowledge toward my future endeavors came about beginning the summer before my final year of college. I was hired as special assistant to Madge Megargee, who was the chief executive of WGBI radio station in Scranton. By that time I knew I was interested in journalism and I was anxious to rub elbows with the news team of WDAU-TV, which shared quarters with WGBI in the basement of the former Prudential Building on Wyoming Avenue, the current home of Scranton Prep. Bill Connolly, a college friend who had just graduated from the university, worked in the art department of the television station. I was fascinated with the mechanics of television, which was quite primitive at the time.

WDAU was owned by WCAU, the Philadelphia Evening Bulletin's broadcast division, which had purchased it some years earlier from the Megargee family.

The two stations shared staff as well as quarters and I have no idea how they sorted it out at the end of the day. Occasionally, I got an opportunity to work on the TV side. WDAU traditionally televised the culmination of the annual novena at St. Ann's Monastery on the west side. The novena was and still is a big deal in Scranton. It attracts untold thousands of Catholics from up and down the line—some of them crawling miles on their knees to demonstrate their piety and devotion to the mother of the Blessed Virgin. It took at least two days to set up for the remote broadcast, hauling huge camera cables and sound wires, as well as erecting scaffolding on which to mount the cameras. Contrast that with the situation today. TV crews show up in a panel truck, record the news event digitally and send it back to the station via collapsible antennas that extend from the back of the truck.

I also had a few opportunities to go out with the camera crews. In those days, the TV photographers used 16 mm Bell & Howell cameras loaded with black and white Tri-X film. Occasionally they used sound film, but it was a big deal to set up the camera and sound equipment, so except for news conferences and other formal occasions most news events were recorded on silent film. News film was developed and edited by cutting and splicing and broadcast in black and white. Color television was a thing of the future.

All of that was much fun and exciting but had nothing to do with my job in the radio station, where my primary responsibility was in assisting with "traffic," the scheduling of commercials. I also got a chance to write and produce a few commercials. But the most important skill I learned in my year there was how to write a business letter, something that comes in handy to this day.

Writing was important to me at that point in life. I had decided to become a journalist and had been accepted by Columbia's Graduate School of Journalism. I did not appreciate that my interest in journalism was based on my experience working on the college paper, The Aquinas. I had been editor of The Aquinas for three semesters and I loved it. What I did not appreciate was that what I loved about The Aquinas was that I was in charge and this time it involved more than myself and a few gas pumps. We had an office, a staff, a budget, a schedule, advertisers with expectations and limitations implied by the publisher, the university, which one ignored at his peril. And then there was the mechanical process of printing the paper, which I found fascinating. I didn't realize that instead of aspiring to be a journalist I should have aspired to be a publisher.

My first real job in journalism came right after college the summer before I enrolled at Columbia. Bill Kiesling had been a firebrand editor of The Aquinas when I was a freshman at the university. After college, he purchased a weekly newspaper in suburban Clarks Summit and later had gone on to work as a reporter at The Scranton Tribune. Wherever Kiesling tread, his presence was felt. In the spring of 1960, he left The Tribune to become press secretary for William W. Scranton, who was running for governor of Pennsylvania. Somehow, I was asked to fill in for him over the summer. Bill may have recruited me based on my acceptance by Columbia. My application certainly was aided by the fact that Edward had been working there as a copy boy and was well liked by the staff.

The Tribune newsroom was an experience made more interesting by the Runyonesque characters who hung out there. It was on the second floor of a building on the east side of Washington Avenue, over the press room and the mechanical department. I was assigned to write obituaries and occasional news stories. There was no real reporting involved, but I did learn the rudiments, which meant spelling everyone's name right. Tom Phillips was the city editor. We called him Tom and he seemed a friendly sort for the most part, but occasionally he showed his temper and you kept your distance if you could. The managing editor was B.B. Powell. We called him Mr. Powell. He was a quiet, dignified man who had little to say to me. And then there was J. Harold Brislin, The Tribune's Pulitzer Prize-winning reporter who hung around the newsroom when he had nothing else to do, slouching on a desk, preening and affecting imperious disdain by rolling a toothpick from side to side in his mouth. Harold had won his Pulitzer Prize for exposing involvement by a local labor union in a bomb blast that destroyed a structure being built by non-union laborers. I was well aware of the details of the case because one of the principal figures involved was a prominent parishioner from Nativity, an usher at the Sunday 10 o'clock mass and, if I recall correctly, a daily communicant, one who in retrospect may have been *non dignus*.

Harold's wife, Jeannie, was a newsroom fixture. She was the society editor and while she was in middle age she dressed and acted like a teen-ager. Chic Feldman was the sports editor. He was the dean of Scranton sports writers and a colorful figure. The University of Scranton had opted for an uninspiring nickname for its sports teams, which officially were called the Royals. Chic preferred the name used by teams that played for the university's predecessor, St. Thomas College, Father's alma mater. So, in the columns of The Tribune, the Royals were referred to as the "Tommies." And then there was Tom Casey and Joe Flannery, good flexible working journalists who could and did cover everything. On large metropolitan dailies they would have been called general assignment reporters. Casey is memorable as the only journalist in Scranton who made an issue of the beating death of a local homosexual man, something that today would be labeled a "hate crime." Tom was genuinely interested in identifying and prosecuting the perpetrators, which was unusual for the time.

Willard Jenkins was somewhat of an enigma. It was clear that he was extremely bright and well read, but he did not seem particularly ambitious—a characteristic of the archetypical newspaperman of the time. But when called upon, Willard could turn into a dynamo of a reporter-writer, churning out take after take of presentable prose, explaining the most complicated story in simple terms, all on deadline. Al Williams was the wire editor, in charge of designing page one, among other things. He ultimately succeeded Mr. Powell as managing editor. There were others, but my memory is dim. What I recall clearly is that none of them felt an obligation to abuse the neophyte on the obit desk.

On the obituary beat I learned the value of getting all basic facts right. I learned that the average person found his or her name in the paper only three times in a lifetime—at birth, marriage and death. I was responsible for the death part. First name, middle initial, last name, age—all were important and had to be right. We fudged on the cause of death, since many folks were reluctant to share that bit of information. We accepted the age specified by the funeral director, knowing that many folks were several years older than reported. It was not uncommon in those days for folks to find themselves trapped in a bogus age due to their having lied years earlier when they purchased life insurance. Anything to save a buck. My news writing was confined mostly to reports of auto accidents in the outlying areas of Northeastern Pennsylvania. It was my duty to check twice a night with the various state police barracks in our circulation area. This was hardly the stuff of Pulitzer Prizes, but it was a start.

I believe I earned $65 a week at The Tribune. It was more money than I had ever earned in my life. Top union scale was $125 a week. I knew that if I stayed at The Tribune for five years I would automatically reach top scale, which I believe was more than Father earned at the time. It crossed my mind that maybe I did not have to go to Columbia. I will be forever grateful that I did not fall prey to the temptation.

16

The Creature

No memoir of a person of Irish descent would be complete without some discussion of the *craythur,* also known as the creature or craytchur. Technically, the creature refers to what the Irish call "strong drink," distilled spirits, most often illegally distilled, what we call "moonshine" in the United States and they call *poteen* in Ireland. I use the term loosely in reference to all alcoholic beverages consumed as lubricants to social discourse and/or for their mind-altering potential. Tom Lavin, a Jungian analyst friend from Chicago, has observed that the Irish lost their spirit during the centuries of occupation and oppression by the English, so they turned to spirits. Nothing is as simple as that, of course, but alcohol is a larger presence among the Irish than in many other ethnic groups.

Alcohol had no place in our home, however, when we were children. Our only exposure was to a mixture of cheap blended whiskey and sugar, administered by mother when we took to our beds, suffering severely from one of the myriad of childhood diseases. It was a vile concoction, designed, I suspect, to chase the offending virus to a more welcoming habitat. Neither Father nor Mother, nor any of our relatives who lived nearby drank alcohol, to my knowledge. There was no suggestion that alcohol in and of itself was immoral, which was the Protestant "Blue Law" mentality. But it was made clear that alcohol could lead to abuse and flagrantly self-destructive behavior.

Drinking was not an issue until high school. During summer vacations, I spent time with Jimmy Harrison, a classmate from the Prep and Johnny Lafferty, who lived across the street from Jimmy and worked with me at Al Bielinski's market. Johnny was a year ahead of us and attended South Catholic High School. Karl Snyder rounded out our group. He lived in the unit block of South Irving Avenue, just south of the Laurel Line tracks, and, therefore, was a neighbor of Jimmy and Johnny. Karl was of German descent and attended the German parish high school, St. Mary's. Why Karl spent time with us is somewhat of a mystery, since we rode him continually, calling him Hans or the Heini (for Heinrich, I suppose) or Nazi. We used words instead of fists, but we weren't too far removed from the thugs who beat up Ralph Falzetti after all, I guess. He took it all good naturedly, just as Ralph smiled as they pummeled his belly.

I don't think alcohol was available in any of our homes except for Karl's. He was German and beer is a staple of the German diet and culture. Neither I nor either of my two Irish friends had tasted beer. We were familiar with it, of course, from the ever-present radio commercials for Standard Tru Age, Stegmaier and Gibbons beer. At the time, Pennsylvania was home to a host of small breweries that made what today would be called boutique beers. Standard was the only brewery in Scranton. Stegmaier and Gibbons were in Wilkes-Barre. We were also familiar with Rolling Rock from Latrobe, PA, near Pittsburgh, and Peals, from New York, which was advertised on Binghamton's Channel 12, the first television station to serve our market. And then there were the national brands. We knew about them but knew nothing of drinking beer.

That was soon to change. One day, Karl brought several "pony" bottles of beer from home and we put them in a spring we knew along the Laurel Line tracks. After a half-hour of chilling we retrieved and opened a bottle, passing it around so each of us could take a swig. I remember wondering how anyone could drink such a vile-tasting substance on a regular basis. Beer then was heavily "hopped," unlike the mass market beers available today. It was bitter and, as I was to learn, is "an acquired taste." It was also a rite of passage. One had achieved some level of maturity and sophistication when he could persuade a merchant to sell him alcohol when the legal drinking age was 21. Bitter or not, forbidden fruits are always in demand.

It wasn't long before we knew who the less scrupulous merchants were. Beer was not difficult to obtain and was particularly available at high school graduation parties. A group of us and several cases of beer made their way to a classmate's cottage at Lake Ariel, where we celebrated our graduation until the following morning. This was after making the rounds of all the standard graduation parties in town. It seems that the liver enzymes in young folks are capable of Herculean effort when challenged by copious volumes of two-carbon fragments.

By that point I had graduated as well to drinking in those bars or tap rooms where I knew I would be admitted. The earliest of these was a modest establishment known as Chappy's. It was on Madison Avenue near Mulberry, just a few blocks from the university. It was not a university hangout, however, and I was not yet a university student. Chappy was an amiable sort and asked no questions. You placed an order and he filled it. The premises were dimly lit and I preferred to sit at one of the tables he had facing the television set. I can recall drinking 16-ounce cans of Pabst Blue Ribbon while watching boxing sponsored by Pabst Blue Ribbon on Channel 12. I was not then and am not now a fight fan, but television was new and captivating. It was reported that some people even watched the test pattern after stations stopped broadcasting for the day.

Captivating or not, I found myself more interested in the small daily dramas played out by the regular patrons, most of whom sat at the bar. Others stood and moved along the bar, telling their tales of woe or glee at each and every stop. There were occasional brief conflicts, but they were defused quickly by Chappy who was always nearby. My recollection is that most folks drank beer, though there was an occasional heavy duty drinker who downed a shot of whiskey with each beer.

At the university, I quickly learned that the preferred watering hole was Andre's and O'Toole's, east of the campus on Mulberry Street. Students could be found there virtually every night, though they had a large following from the neighborhood as well. One occasional customer was Mr. Powell, managing editor of The Tribune, who occasionally stopped in for a beer on his way home from work. One thing they had that Chappy did not was food. I was a regular there, along with Bill Connolly, John Rafferty and Jim Harrison. We were college boys now, so we no longer called him Jimmy. We all were active in the various clubs at the university.

Our habit was to head for O'Toole's, as it was known, after finishing whatever we were doing at the university, which ranged from working on the student newspaper to practicing for an upcoming play or attending the monthly meeting of the Student Council. We gathered in a booth and reviewed the activities of the day, the state of the world, the state of the university or some other topic of interest. All of us had been trained and were experienced in debate, so we often took opposing side of an issue, whether or not we truly believed in our position. It was intellectual exercise, mental masturbation, so to speak, but it was fun and we all enjoyed it. I was to learn as I made my way in the world that such aggressive argumentation made most folks uncomfortable, but at that time and in that place, where there continued to be a whole lot of nothin' goin' on, it was a welcome diversion.

Our over-all alcohol consumption on those occasions was modest, I am sure, for two reasons: We were all on limited budgets for one thing, and we had to get up for class in the morning. I can't recall missing class due to a hangover, even on those few occasions when there definitely was over consumption, such as an unanticipated victory by our basketball team. Very memorable was the Royals' victory over Seton Hall when the Pirates were ranked number one in the nation. O'Toole's really rocked that night. Such occasions really challenged our liver enzymes.

The beverage of choice remained beer throughout college, according to my best recollection. That doesn't mean we were totally ignorant of distilled spirits. It may have been partly a matter of availability and cost. Beer was available from many sources and was relatively inexpensive—the choice of the common man, so to speak. Spirits and wines were available only at state liquor stores where the civil servants behind the counter had no incentive to look the other way when an under-age college student showed up. I particularly remember one encounter with the creature in the form of Seagram's 7 blended whiskey mixed with 7Up—the classic seven and seven. The mixer totally masked the revolting taste of the cheap blend and the drinks just slid down, much to my chagrin an hour of so later when the alcohol overload took effect and I found myself embracing the porcelain goddess. Since then, I have generally avoided mixed drinks, especially those made with sweet, carbonated mixers.

I have come to believe that those college students who choose to drink consume prodigious amounts of alcohol, amounts that in later life would make them totally dysfunctional. Perhaps college in and of itself is a dysfunctional experience. If that is true, we were too busy at the time to notice.

Among the activities that kept us busy was the Intercollegiate Conference on Government conducted each year in Harrisburg. Delegations from colleges all across the state participated in some form of model government exercise. Most years it was a model legislature and the various regions in the state posted a slate of candidates for the various legislative offices. There was always a lot of horse trading and partying prior to the election and everyone had a good time. The officers who were elected presided over the general sessions of the body and, therefore, had to have a good grasp of parliamentary procedure.

In 1960, my senior year, the conference was scheduled to be a model nominating convention. That added excitement because Sen. John F. Kennedy of Massachusetts was a candidate for the Democratic nomination and I was the candidate of the Northeast Region to be speaker of the assembly. I was determined to run a good campaign on my behalf and that of Senator Kennedy.

A major feature of the political maneuvering prior to the vote for speaker was the operation of hospitality suites on behalf of candidates by the five regions throughout the state. Since I was the candidate of the university it would our responsibility to operate the suite of the Northeast Region. Beer was always plentiful at these parties and we decided ours would be memorable in that regard. I had a fairly substantial nest egg at the time because I continued to work thorough school and was careful with expenses. So, it was well within my means to purchase 40 cases of Gibbons beer, which was delivered to my home and stored in our half of the garage. My age was not a factor at that point because I was 22, just a few months from graduation. What was legal was not always acceptable in the family, however. Given my entire family's wariness of alcohol I was not certain how this would be received. Surprisingly, no one objected, even the sainted Nellie, which mother interpreted as a special fondness for me. I think she was fond of us all. I had very little choice in the matter, however, since the beer had to be delivered somewhere and the distributor was unlikely to truck it to Harrisburg.

That fell to us. We rented a truck, loaded the beer and were off to the state capital. What we had not counted on is that the hotel was unwilling to let us schlep the beer through the lobby and up to the hospitality suite. Not to worry, the Scranton boys were nothing if not resourceful. The hotel did have a loading dock and a freight elevator, so we took that route. Instead of just passing out the beer as it came out of the case, we affixed labels with my campaign message to the cans. For several days, cans with the Carden labels could be found in the most obscure corners of that hotel. But the beer was not enough to carry the election. Frank McDonnell, my classmate from the Prep, was in charge of the campaign and struck a bargain with another region; its candidate for speaker would be elected but all other convention offices would be filled with candidates from our region. That made me vice speaker. It was the best we could do and I was pleased.

My recollection is that the proceedings became boisterous quite quickly since many of the delegations were passionate supporters of one candidate or another. Election politics is much more contentious that debates over legislative issues. In the face of an unruly assembly, the speaker seemed uncertain. She lacked the necessary knowledge of and facility with Roberts Rules of Order to control the debate, so she yielded the podium. There I was, in charge again. Some things were meant to be. The speaker is supposed to be neutral but that was not in my nature. I had come there to have the assembly endorse the candidacy of John F. Kennedy and I was not about to be denied.

Ultimately, it came down to a vote of the assembly and Kennedy won handily, despite multiple unsuccessful maneuvers to prevent the vote or to prolong debate. Genevieve Blatt, a long-standing political official in Pennsylvania who had been a loyal supporter of and adviser to the Intercollegiate Conference on Government was not pleased. Genevieve, who had a balcony seat during the proceedings, made it clear that she was not amused that I had not been totally neutral in presiding over the proceedings, ultimately paving the way for a Kennedy endorsement. She was a strong supporter of Adlai Stevenson. Apparently she was not concerned that if Stevenson had been nominated he undoubtedly would have been destined to challenge Harold Stassen as the archetypically pathetic perennial candidate.

Genevieve's displeasure was of little concern to our delegation. We had unleashed the creature in support of our campaigns. We had won one and lost one, but in losing we were put in a position to effect a win. That was something worth drinking to.

17

Music and Photography

The Carden children were all expected to learn a musical instrument. We started with the piano. Lessons were given by Sister Victoire in a side room in the convent. I have no idea whether Sister was a good or incompetent teacher. What I do know is that I was an incompetent student. I had no talent and less interest in the instrument, particularly since it required constant practice, which took me away from the radio adventure serials in the afternoon. Edward was much better at the piano and learned well enough to play some complicated pieces years later when those convent sessions with Sister Victoire had faded from memory.

Next came the violin. I don't recall whose idea that was but it could have been mine. Back to Sister Victoire. She was either multitalented or merely willing to tackle anything. I learned later that children my age who began to learn the violin were given child-size instruments. Mine was a full-size instrument, which made it difficult to maneuver through the scales. This is not to imply that the size of the instrument destroyed a budding career as a concert violinist. I was as untalented with the violin as I was with the piano. And a violin in the hands of a poor student is more nuisance than musical instrument. When I petitioned my parents to quit I believe they were relieved.

There was a hiatus of several years while the family concentrated its musical expectations on the twins. Then in seventh grade came word that the newly opened South Catholic High School was forming a marching band and we were eligible to participate. I chose to play the alto saxophone. Bob Davey, a classmate who later went with me to the Prep, chose trumpet. I think the school provided some very basic lessons, but if we were to really learn the instrument we would have to take private lessons. Sister Victoire was no longer in the picture. If she had been I doubt I would have proceeded.

My instructor was Mario Chemi, a very talented man who, among other things, had been hired as the band director at South Catholic. In retrospect, I don't believe I had any real talent for the saxophone either, but Mario trained me to the point that I was able to perform a solo at the first South Catholic band concert. I was in seventh grade and I was first saxophone in a high school band. It was almost as good as being in charge. There may have been a second and a third saxophone but I have no recollection of who they might have been. I learned to read music well enough to play marches and other straightforward tunes, but I was never going to be a musician.

That did not prevent me from continuing to play the saxophone, no matter how poorly. At the Prep, we had an opportunity to play in the University of Scranton marching band. The band director: Mario Chemi. Who else? It was fun traveling to out-of-town football games and rubbing elbows with the college students. When we marched and played at home games at Memorial Stadium, there was always cider and donuts waiting for us in the Green Room of Old Main after our march back across the Mulberry Street Bridge. I could not wait to grow up and this was a step in that direction. But I was no longer first saxophone, even at the Prep. Jack Kraniak, a classmate from up the line was a really talented sax player, good enough to play weekends with several dance bands in the area.

The football marching band was unemployed for much of the year, but I played often enough to maintain a competence level adequate to the task. But there would be no more solo performances. I was strictly a warm body who carried a funny-looking horn and blew it when called on.

That skill, no matter how primitive, came in handy when I matriculated to the university, where all first- and second-year classmen were obliged to take military science—ROTC. We wore dress uniforms to class every Wednesday and the "cadet corps" marched off to the Watrous Armory for even more marching on Wednesday afternoons. Ironically, the only contingent that did not march every Wednesday was the ROTC marching band. We marched in parades and other events where the corps was put on display. At all other times, band practice under the direction of Mario Chemi was deemed more important than routine marching. I suppose folks figured that a marching band would know how to march when called upon to do so.

When my ROTC obligation expired at the end of my sophomore year, my days as a saxophonist came to an end as well. I was convinced I had better things to do and even forgot where the saxophone was stored. When I tried to recover it two years later I could not find it. Mother was not amused.

While music turned out to be a useful skill, limited that it was, I never gained a true appreciation for it. Even today, I rarely listen to music, even in the car, where I prefer National Public Radio. I guess I am more fact-driven than artistic, even though I test out as right-brain dominant, I guess my artistic inclinations are satisfied in other ways.

One of them is photography. I have been interested in photography and image manipulation since high school. I vividly recall the first time I saw a photograph emerge on a blank piece of photosensitive paper in a bath of developer in Paul Antal's dark room. I knew immediately that I had to learn more about this fascinating process. My first camera was a Yashica-mat, a twin lens reflex imitation of the famed German Rollieflex. The Yashica cost less than $100, considerably less than the Rollie and, therefore, within my budget. It took 120 mm film, each roll of which produced twelve 2 ¼ X 2 ¼-inch negatives.

The next step was a dark room. Luckily for me there were two unused fruit cellars in the basement under 222 Prospect, which was accessible from 224 via a door in the wall. They were called fruit cellars, I believe, because mother stored "canned" fruits and vegetables there during the war. It's hard to understand why the process is called "canning" because it does not use cans. A more accurate descriptor would be "jarring," since it involves preservation of prepared fruits or vegetables in large-mouth Mason jars that had been sterilized with boiling water. They were sealed with paraffin wax under screw caps and stored in a dark place, the ideal site for a dark room. The war was only a memory when I decided to create a dark room, so the space was available.

Darkness was the easy part. The rooms were not light tight but as long as no one turned on the cellar lights it would do. I did erect a few dark curtains to protect the most sensitive parts of the process. Somewhere I acquired an enlarger and pans for developer, stop and fixer. Photo paper exposed under the enlarger was immersed in the developer until an image emerged. It then was dipped in the stop, ascetic acid, which terminated the development process. It was then plunged into the fixer for several minutes to fix the image to the paper and made it impervious to further exposure to light. The paper could then be dried, which gave you the final product. If it were dried by placing it on a clean chromium plate exposed to heat it would dry with a glossy finish. Eventually, I purchased am electric drier that could handle two large chromium plates capable of holding a total of eight 8 X 10-inch prints at a time. Print development could be carried on successfully under illumination by a "safe" light, which allowed me to monitor the prints as they developed.

Film development was another matter, however. Any stray light could fog the film, so film development had to be carried on in absolute darkness, not always easy in the fruit cellar. Roll film was developed by threading it on reels and then placing the reels in stainless steel tubes with light-tight tops through which you could pour the chemicals in and out. The threading and loading process could be done in a light-tight sack with arm openings. Then you could pour developer through the lid for the specified period of time, followed by the stop and fixer. After a few minutes in the fixer you could remove the reels and inspect the film. It was a one-shot process and if you ruined the film there was no recovery. However, in the enlargement and print development process there were many maneuvers you could employ to compensate for imperfections in the negative. I was limited to black-and-white film and prints because color film processing required strict temperature control, which was impossible in the fruit cellar. It was also too costly and since I was most interested in photos for publication locally I had no need for color.

As with most projects I undertake, I read everything I could find about photography. I subscribed to several photography magazines and bought many books. Among the books were a few that included photographs of scantily clad women by Peter Gowland. He made it seem that you could prowl the streets of any city and find beautiful women who would be more than willing to shed most of their clothes for the honor of having their image recorded on your film for posterity. This, of course, was pure fantasy, but the pictures were interesting and I knew them well. Years later, I was surprised to find many of them in a newly published book of anatomy for medical students. I was delighted with the book, of course, since I found the traditional approach to the most basic medical subject to be atrociously boring. I made the mistake of writing an article praising the news book and stirred up a firestorm of criticism from feminists. That is an interesting story but is outside the scope of this work.

My first published picture was a product of serendipity. Word spread through the neighborhood that Sophia Loren was visiting relatives. The Italian actress was a box-office sensation at the time and I was optimistic that if I could get a picture of her visiting in Scranton one of the newspapers would publish it. I was right. I don't remember where her relatives lived or who they were, but I did find her and she agreed to be photographed with several relatives. I remember being struck by how large she was—a very imposing subject. Unfortunately, the photo was not impressive but it was good enough to be published the following morning in The Tribune—my first byline in a commercial publication. I think about that time I was convinced I was going to be a photojournalist.

If that was my goal I needed a new camera. The only photojournalists I knew in those days were the photographers for the two daily newspapers. They did not carry Yashica-mats. Their camera of choice was the Speed Graphic, generally known as the "press camera," the work horse of news photography, which exposed 4 X 5-inch sheet film carried in two-sided "slides" that were exposed one side at a time—a very slow process that dated back to Matthew Brady. Several improvements had been made since the Civil War and the cumbersome device could be manipulated reasonably rapidly by an experienced photographer. When I went to buy my Speed Graphic I found that it was no longer made. My option was a used camera or a new, more sophisticated Super Graphic, which, of course, is what I bought. Improvements in film and flash bulbs had made the focal plane shutter in the Speed Graphic obsolete, so it had been eliminated from the Super Graphic, which also had controls that were easier to operate than in its predecessor.

Acquisition of a press camera required some upgrading of the dark room. Instead of developing the film sheets in a stainless steel tube, they were placed in individual hangers and suspended in developer before being advanced through the stop to the fixer, and could be inspected under the safe light. Luckily for me, the equipment was inexpensive. Used battery cases served as containers for the developer, stop and fixer. A dozen hangers were adequate for my needs. I did have to upgrade the light protection, however, since I could not protect the sheet film from ambient light once I removed it from the slides.

The press camera served me for years as an official badge for entry to sites of news events and other happenings of interest. In those days, reporters and photographers did not carry IDs around their necks and anyone carrying something that looked like a Speed Graphic was presumed to be representing a publication. I used it throughout my college years to take photographs for the student newspaper and occasionally for the year book. Later, in the military, it served me very well. When the colonel learned that I could write and take pictures I was never again expected to carry a gun, despite my primary MOS (military occupation specialty) of heavy weapons infantryman. In medical school, I earned what Mother would call "good money" as editor of the yearbook during my final two years and supplied most of the photographs. By that time the technology had improved and I used a single-lens reflex Minolta 35 mm camera.

But as usual, mother was right. I had taken so many photographs for so many different purposes over the years that despite the availability of the most sophisticated camera equipment my interest waned. I had done so much photography that I became bored. The cameras lay idle in the closet as I pursued other interests. In recent years I have resurrected my interest somewhat and manipulate images almost daily using Adobe Photoshop, the most sophisticated photo editing software available. I've even bought a state-of-the-art digital Nikon. Are these the first signs of a second childhood? Don't answer that question.

18

The Pack Phenomenon

With the transition from Nativity School to the Prep, daily exposure to those of the opposite gender ceased. That did not expunge them from our minds, however, as described earlier. It just made it harder for us to socialize with or date girls since we encountered them only in controlled environments or when our paths crossed at some school-sponsored event such as a basketball game or dance. On such occasions, the girls traveled in packs, as did the boys. For any one-on-one discourse, one had to leave his pack, enter the female pack, select a target and attempt to initiate meaningful conversation. The same held true at informal dances, where you had to enter the pack and ask your target to honor you with a dance. A refusal was humiliating. Under most circumstances, it seemed safer and more comfortable to remain with your pack of origin and discuss the relative merits of various members of the female pack with your mates.

And then there was the issue of transportation. In the first two years of high school, we were all too young to qualify for a driver's license. Mothers may have been willing to drive their sons and dates to semi-formal dances, which, after all, were considered reasonably important events. But they were not about to routinely schlep junior as he went on the prowl. So, aside from semi-formal dances and exposure to the packs of girls at basketball games and informal dances, we had to depend on the telephone. After attending my first semi-formal affair with Irene Sexton, I remember spending a lot of time on the telephone with her. But she lived in Dunmore and I lived on the other side of town. It never occurred to me that I could take the streetcar to the end of the line, as my grandfather had, and then walked to her home. Relationships have to be nurtured and the telephone didn't cut it.

I know that there were quite a few dances at Marywood and reciprocal affairs at the Prep and I know that I went to them all, but have no recollection of with whom. That did not mean I disliked my dates or that I failed to have a good time at these events, but no ongoing relationship developed. That would not occur until my junior year, when, coincidentally I had a driver's license and periodic access to the family car.

Folks who have known me for a long time have commented that I seem attracted to women with red hair, which is a fair assessment dating back to my fascination in the fourth grade with a neighborhood siren named Audrey Cox. It is said that red hair among the Irish is a trait linked to genes contributed by the Vikings, who originally raided and pillaged Ireland but eventually settled in and intermarried with the natives. Analysis of my mitochondrial DNA suggests some Viking lineage. That may be totally irrelevant, but I know that I find women with red hair attractive. Patricia Kelley had red hair and freckles as well—a real colleen. She was the older sister of Gene Kelley, the president of our class and a personal friend. And, oddly enough, she did not travel with the Marywood pack. She attended St. Ann's Academy in Wilkes-Barre, an exclusive Catholic high school for girls operated by the Sisters of Christian Charity. It was Wilkes-Barre's equivalent of Marywood Seminary. Maybe it was the fact she came alone to watch her brother play basketball that facilitated my meeting her. I did not have to brave the dreaded pack to open a conversation.

Whatever the explanation, I have no detailed recollection of how I came to know Tia, as she was known, but with access to a car I had the means as well as the motivation to pursue a relationship. The Kelleys lived in Exeter, a town on the east side of the Susquehanna River south of Pittston and north of Kingston. That alone made access to a car essential. Gene and Tia had two sisters, Mary and Annie. All the Kelley children and their mother had red hair. Shortly after I started dating Tia, the family was devastated by the death of their father. That cast a pall over things for a brief period but Tia quickly let me know that she wanted to continue seeing me. Those were heady times and I was sure we were in love. We probably were, but we were also young and naïve. That summer I worked the night shift at Bobby Brier's gas station, so I had plenty of opportunities to visit Tia and her family at their summer home on the Susquehanna at Harding. I made the drive from Harding to Prospect Avenue and Moosic Street in record time. Our relationship seemed to be getting closer by the day and I was ecstatic.

Tia started college that fall at Marywood. I never occurred to me that might make a difference and it didn't—at first. I can only surmise what might have happened. By and large, college girls simply did not waste their time with high school boys. And college girls were likely to explain that to other college girls. Before long the relationship was over, and I was heartbroken. I was also angry. I think I was in a major funk for the rest of my senior year. After all, I was not used to setbacks and was not prepared for my love to be unrequited. In retrospect, my expectations were unrealistic. I was not as sophisticated as I thought I was. In later life, after analysis of my fantasies and recurrent dreams, Tom Lavin, my Jungian friend, suggested that I meet all of the criteria for the *Puer Aeternus* (eternal boy) archetype. I may be the eternal boy, but if I ever met a *Puella Aeternus* it was Tia. That trait was captivating when I was a high school senior, but the failure of our relationship to progress to ultimate fulfillment may have been a blessing. *Puer* and *Puella* together, it seems to me, is a surefire recipe for disaster.

That, of course, was not apparent to me at the time. Somehow, I got through the rest of the school year. My disappointment did not impair enthusiastic participation in the graduation festivities. College was looming and was sure to offer the opportunity for new and better relationships. I was down, but never out. The university sponsored dances every Friday night in the Green Room, which was really the ground floor of Old Main on Wyoming Avenue. At the Green Room dances, the pack phenomenon continued to be observed. But we were older and more experienced, less fearful of being rejected. Most of the girls were willing to dance with just about anyone. After all, it was just a dance. And, unlike the South Catholic square dances, frontal contact was the norm—even what one might term aggressive frontal contact.

I recall meeting a very nice young woman named Mary at a Green Room dance and we dated for awhile. Mary did not have red hair, but her auburn locks were close enough to attract my attention. I found her to be smart and genuine. She worked in an office in Scranton. That concerned me in that I knew Mother expected me to date college girls. She was a strong believer in education. I continued to see Mary and she helped me with some of my college assignments. Then as now, my typing was limited to the hunt and peck method. Typing was a subject so mundane it was not taught at the Prep, which put us at a distinct advantage when term papers were due. Those were the days before word processors with automatic correction and spell check. If you made an error it was a big deal, particularly if you were making carbon copies of the original. Mary was an excellent typist. She took the chicken scratch that I prepared and virtually effortlessly produced a professional looking document.

I liked Mary. Her typing was a bonus. Unfortunately, I was indiscreet in sharing news of this unanticipated side benefit of my new girlfriend with a classmate. There was plenty of competition in the male pack, and any perceived weakness, any deviation from the norm was instantly pounced upon. My friends began to ride me constantly about "Mary term paper." I regretted ever telling anyone about Mary's typing, but continued dating her despite the razzing. As I said, I liked her. Who knows what might have happened, but one night I took her home several hours after her curfew. The door was locked. She had to ring the doorbell to get in. I stood there with her on the porch, expecting to undergo a barrage of criticism from her father. What I did not expect was that as he emerged from the upstairs stairwell it was clear he was nude. I did not know at that time that many folks prefer to sleep in the nude. It shocked me. I knew that he was of a different cultural background, but what kind of man would not only sleep in the nude but come to the door in that state to let his daughter into her home? I liked Mary, but I began to wonder what this "natural man" might do to me if he perceived that I was not doing right by his daughter. That was the end of the relationship. I heard years later that Mary had married another university graduate. I suspect she is a good wife and mother.

While college girls did not as a matter of course hang around with mere high school boys, college men were not above dating high school girls, and I was no exception. Somehow, I met and liked a girl from St. Ann's Academy, where Tia Kelley had been a student two years earlier. Pat Thomas did not have red hair. She was a brunette with long, straight tresses extending two-thirds of the way down her back and bangs in front. I was attracted to long hair as well. (Caution, *Puer* on the prowl). Pat was a classmate of Mary Kelley, whom I presume arranged for us to meet. I was still friendly with all members of the Kelley family so that would not have been unusual. Pat lived in Wilkes-Barre and if I was to see her on a regular basis I would need a car. Fortunately, John Adams had a light lime green 1949 Studebaker convertible and somehow it came to be mine—my very own car. The Studebaker had an interesting design, with both the front and the back tapering to a point, somewhat suggestive of a bullet, if you had an active imagination. Folks commented that you could not tell if the car was coming or going. My personal bulletmobile made scores of trips to Wilkes-Barre and back.

Pat had a friend whose name escapes me. I introduced her to Joe O'Hara, a Korean vet who was finishing up at the university. Joe was known by his friends as "Neffie," short for nefarious. He was serious about many things but was quite mischievous and lots of fun. He liked Pat's friend and we were a foursome for quite awhile. A major dating activity at the time was to attend movies at outdoor theaters. Some folks were said to actually watch the movies. The back seat of that Studebaker was quite cramped, but "Neffie" made do. Eventually the Studebaker broke down and for some reason I was determined to fix it myself. Several months later, it was towed out of our driveway to the scrap yard. Some things are best left to others.

Perhaps it was the lack of wheels or perhaps the relationship simply had run its course, but I stropped seeing Pat. She visited me at home several years later after I had graduated from the university. She had moved from Wilkes-Barre to California and considered herself quite sophisticated. She was surprised and, I believe, impressed to learn that I was heading off that fall to New York, which trumps California every time. It was not clear why she stopped but it was my impression that she wanted to see how I had turned out.

I continued to be friendly with "Neffie," who was responsible for my unhappy introduction to seven and sevens. He also introduced me to the Ukrainian Social Club on Wyoming Avenue, where members could drink legally on Sundays, as well as other days, of course. He and I both became members—Irishmen who were honorary Ukrainians. At the end of my freshman year, "Neffie" called me and asked if I was interested in going to the senior prom at Marywood College. I thought that I might be biting off more than I could comfortably chew, since I knew any girl who was graduating from college had to be several years older than I. It also crossed my mind that any girl who could not get a date on her own for her senior prom may be less than desirable. But what the hell, it was only a dance.

"Neffie" and consulted about which of the girls we would pair with for the dance. Sight unseen, I agreed to escort Terry and "Neffie" took Lois. Both girls were boarding students at Marywood, which partially explained their lack of a date for the prom. They were staying with their parents for the weekend at the Hotel Casey, so we did not have to venture to the campus, which was aggressively patrolled by the nuns at all times. Curfews were rigorously enforced. Hotel Casey was a much better option. I don't remember much about the dance but I do remember that Terry attacked me in the back seat afterward. It was my turn to be in the back seat with "Neffie" driving. She apparently was taking advantage of this opportunity to sample what had been so vigorously denied by the nuns during her four years at Marywood. Her needs were such that I was not about to deny her. Whatta guy!

While there were many good intentions expressed as I left Terry off at her room, I never saw her again. "Neffie," however, continued to date Lois. He finished at the university and headed to New York where he got a master's degree in social work from Fordham. "Neffie" and Lois eventually married and I visited them at their home on Long Island during the year I spent at Columbia. Blind dates sometimes pan out.

As I reflect on this series of tales about relationships during my early years, it occurs to me that they all occurred outside the various packs. That may not have been a coincidence. Males and females traveled in packs for mutual support, but the pack phenomenon was a deterrent to free social intercourse. There was a risk for one to leave his or her pack to initiate activity with someone in a pack of the opposite gender. At the Green room dances that didn't seem to matter much since the young men and women seemed to mix freely even if they were committed at the time to a relatively exclusive relationship with someone else.

So it was that I was attracted to Marion Whitney, a red-haired Marywood student. I knew that she was a graduate of St. Patrick's High School on the West side and was a year behind me. I began to notice her during my sophomore year at the university. I knew that she had a boyfriend but did not consider that an obstacle to asking her to dance. I was stunned when she invariably refused. At first I thought she simply did not know who I was—the quintessential Big Man on Campus (BMOC). She could not have appreciated that I was a young man with a bright future—the big job out of town. I presumed that when she found how just who I was she would be happy to dance. After all, it was just a dance. I was confident that if and when she and I danced she would be captivated by my charm and we might pursue a relationship. I may have been confident, but it never happened. Could it be that she knew exactly who I was and simply was uninterested? Unthinkable! At any rate, she was steadfast in her refusal to dance and I continued to wonder why. Ultimately, I graduated from the university without ever dancing with Marion.

As Mike Ditka, the Hall of Fame tight end for the Chicago Bears might say, "Life deals many unexpected cards." A little over two years after that graduation, Marion and I were married. But that story is beyond the scope of this memoir.

19

Puer at the Wheel

The horseless carriage is a major symbol of the modern age. With the end of World War II, the automotive industry, which had been engaged in manufacturing tanks and airplanes turned its attention to meeting pent-up consumer demand. Autos, which had been boxes on wheels, began to get streamlined and attractive. Styles changed almost annually, so it was a challenge for us to recognize the various makes and models on the roads. But recognize them we did because the automobile for a young man was a symbol of freedom. In Pennsylvania, it was a freedom denied to those under 16 years old.

When I turned 16, my highest priority was getting a driver's license. I was expected to pay the fee, which I earned by setting pins in the bowling alley at the Catholic Youth Center. Those were the day before automatic pin setters. We sat in the well at the end of the alley and waited for the bowler to hurl the ball toward the pins. We then rolled the ball back to the front of the alley and collected the downed pins, inserting them into appropriate slots in the pin setter. Since very few bowlers knocked over all the pins with the initial bowl, we repeated the process for most frames. Any remaining pins left standing after two tries remained in place as we brought the pinsetter down to set up for the next bowler. Since there were 10 frames in a game, there was the potential for 20 repetitions of the process for each bowler, and since there were usually four bowlers to a team there was the potential for 80 total repetitions. Since each human pinsetter was responsible for two alleys, we could look forward to a potential 160 repetitions without an opportunity to catch our breath. Those few occasions when someone bowled a strike, knocking down all 10 pins with the first ball, did not significantly affect the work, which I was grateful to get.

The Catholic Youth Center, in and of itself, was an interesting building. Nominally built to meet the needs of the youth of diocese, it was what one might expect of a building built under the direction of a bishop who was not supposed to have any children and who never acknowledged them if he did. The only feature of the building that served the needs of the young people of Scranton was the indoor swimming pool, which was popular during the long winters. Otherwise, the structure mainly served the needs of adults. The local professional basketball team played there, as did the University of Scranton Royals. There were concerts and other entertainment for adults. There was one major high school basketball tournament every year. Otherwise, the Catholic youth Center was a boondoggle as far as the Catholic youth were concerned.

Once I obtained my license, the objective became access to the family car. At that point I was traveling mostly in the company of John Lafferty, Jim Harrison and Karl Snyder. Each of our families had one car, which was in varying demand for adult transportation requirements. When the car was idle, it became an object of desire. We plotted together when we might "get" our respective family cars and what we would do, where we would go when we did. On those occasions, generally all four of would pile into whosever car we had and we tooled around town, honking at our friends. This was a rite of passage. I gained an unexpected advantage with my parents in the quest for the family car when I competed in and won the Scranton Junior Chamber of Commerce Roadeo, a contest of driving skill. In the Roadeo, you were required to navigate an obstacle course without knocking over any of the orange cones and were required to demonstrate skill in parallel parking. I can't recall how or why I entered but when I won and had my picture published in the following day's paper, I was convinced that it had been proven incontrovertibly that I was one of the most skilled drivers in town. I think it may have given Mother and Father full confidence that they were entrusting the family chariot to a competent operator.

Their confidence was bolstered further on a trip to visit Aunt Gert and her family in Hamburg, PA, near Reading. The route took us through Wilkes-Barre and Hazleton, then over the mountains to Tamaqua (which some folks pronounced tow-MAH-kway) and on to Hamburg. These visits were generally day trips. We left early in the morning and returned late at night. On this occasion, the visit was marked by the beginning of heavy rainfall that I believe was associated with a hurricane. Hurricanes rarely affected Pennsylvania, so we were not concerned. But on the way back we encountered multiple detours due to washed out bridges and other calamities related to the storm, which continued unabated. I drove all the way home. Father apparently did not consider this a threat to his manhood.

In fact, I think he was pleased that I was willing and able to endure the hours of stress and strain finding my way home over totally unfamiliar terrain.

I had a great interest in access to our 1950 Plymouth because I had met an attractive young lady from Carbondale and we seemed simpatico. The Plymouth gave me an opportunity to explore the potential for a relationship. There was only one hitch. The girl's older brother was the captain and star of the hated St. Rose of Lima High School basketball team, which was Prep's nemesis in the Catholic League. That quickly proved to be an irreconcilable impediment to a relationship and the afternoon excursions to Carbondale ceased, but not before I and my passengers experimented with high-speed highway travel. Sometimes I awaken at night after a nightmare during which the Plymouth crashes on the Scranton-Carbondale Highway. At the time we thought nothing of it, but it was reckless behavior that might or could have ended in tragedy.

The family car also provided transportation for dates, which were memorable events, even though there wasn't much to do besides visits to the outdoor movie theaters and the drive-in restaurants. Those were the days before McDonalds and modern fast food. Kay Hoffman ran a drive-in restaurant in Moosic on the road to Wilkes-Barre. It was a gathering place for years for young adults. Drive-in restaurants were not drive-through restaurants. In a way, they resembled the drive-in theaters. You pulled your car into an available parking space and an attendant took your order, bringing your food on a tray that attached to your window, just as the speaker attached to your window at the drive-in movie. Occasionally you took a date to a traditional restaurant where you sat at a table or in a booth and ordered from a menu. Karl Snyder was so impressed with his first date at such a restaurant that he reported to his buddies that he told the girl when they had been seated that "she could have anything she wanted—hamburger…anything." We never let him forget that one. It is a line I use to this day.

Automobile crashes were not unknown among our acquaintances. Bobby Naughton, the hero of my childhood, was severely injured in a crash in the 300 block of Prospect Avenue. After a lengthy recovery, he walked with a limp. Our 1957 Plymouth was totaled one evening when I was driving west on Mulberry Street. Someone shot out from a side street and struck me amidships in what today would be called a T-bone. There was no seat belt or air bags in the car, but luckily I walked away. The Plymouth was replaced briefly with a Nash, made by American Motors. It was an elegant car, but had a cracked block, which led to a confrontation between Father and the dealer.

I have a vivid memory of one automobile crash. Patricia Palumbo was the daughter of a very successful florist in Dunmore. He purchased a brand new 1957 Chevy Bel Air coupe for Patricia for her graduation from Dunmore High School. The '57 Chevy with its tail fins, hooded headlights, wraparound windshield and flashy styling, has become a classic. For us, it was a cool muscle car. As Patricia tooled around town she turned lots of heads. She was often accompanied by Jeannie Early, a redhead to whom I was attracted, of course. Jeannie was a nursing student at the Mercy Hospital. All nursing students were thought to be "hot" because of their comfortable familiarity with bodily functions and their regimentation and isolation by the nuns, who seemed determined to preserve their virginity.

One summer evening Jim Harrison and Don Mauro, a fellow Prep graduate, and I met Jeannie and Patricia and we all wound up in Patricia's car headed to Moosic Lake. Mauro was driving. I believe Harrison and I were in the back seat with Jeannie. The road to Moosic Lake was an imperfectly maintained serpentine course. We managed to make it to the lake, where there were no public facilities, as I recall. One might ask why we went there. If there was a reason it is lost to memory. But there we did go and then turned around for the return trip, which is forever embedded in my memory.

Mauro had a reputation as a thrill seeker and he certainly was true to form that night. He gunned the fuel-injected V-8 and we tore down the Moosic Lake Road, careening around turns with tires squealing, tossing the back seat passengers from side to side. Eventually we came to a curve around which we would not careen. I still have nightmares of the roadside bank looming closer and closer in the headlights and the sound of crunching metal as we slammed into the bank. I found myself outside of the car, relatively unscathed. None of the others was moving. There was an odor of gasoline but no flames. Frank Jordan recalls that I was particularly chagrined that one of the Scranton newspapers reported that "young Carden was found wandering near the wreckage." In my own mind I acted decisively, flagging down a passing motorist and asking him to get help.

I have no recollection of which rescue service responded but I do recall it took quite awhile for an ambulance to arrive. That was not unusual for the time. We were about 20 years from the development of sophisticated emergency response systems.

At that time I was not qualified to offer a critique and have no recollection of how they performed. What I do know is that we were all transported to Scranton State General Hospital, which was the only institution in town with a doctor on duty 24 hours a day. Consequently, the state hospital handled the bulk of auto accidents in the region. Patients brought to any other hospital had to wait for a doctor to be called and to make his way to the emergency room to provide evaluation and treatment. It was a primitive arrangement, but it was common at that time.

All four of my friends were admitted in serious condition. Jim Harrison was in a coma for weeks. It was a real mess. I could not believe that I had not been hurt. I was certain the doctor must be missing something. If he did, it had no lingering effect because other than a couple of chipped teeth I had no residual effects of the crash—another near miss attributed to my guardian angel. Father came to the hospital to take me home. He demonstrated his wisdom by insisting that I drive. He was concerned that the terrifying experience I had just survived might intimidate me into giving up driving. I don't think that would have happened, but his preventive strategy says a lot about him.

I still recall how embarrassed Mother and Father were when an insurance adjustor came to our home to make a settlement of any claim I might have for damages. A value was placed on the chipped teeth and the potential for future dental work. Mother and Father seemed reluctant to accept the settlement. Folks in those days did not expect to profit from their misfortunes. Ultimately, I did require a root canal and crown, so many years later that the cost of the procedure dwarfed the meager settlement Mother and Father were reluctant to accept. But that didn't really matter, I was essentially uninjured. My only regret was that I never got to find out if Jeannie Early really was "hot," which undoubtedly was just another in an endless list of fantasies.

Despite the Moosic Lake road experience, I continued to love to drive. And the bigger the conveyance the better I liked it. I guess that is a male thing. At the university, the drama club participated in one-act play competitions annually. I volunteered to drive the sets and other necessary paraphernalia to Baltimore and New York City for these events. At that time you did not need any special license or demonstration of competence to drive mid-size cargo trucks. As I recall Frank Jordan accompanied me on these excursions and we managed to get there and return without mishap. Young men consider themselves invincible and a *puer* looking down at the world from the cab of a truck fears nothing.

20

Athletics

Athletic events seem to have a compelling hold on the male psyche. In season, many men can be found in front of the television set, feet propped up and beer close at hand, watching sporting events. Particularly popular seem to be football and basketball, as well as the great American pastime, baseball. In recent years, NASCAR racing has become quite popular as well. As substitutes for war and physical combat, these events play a valuable social role, but their peculiar hold on the male of the species is fascinating.

As we have seen, athletics played little role in my elementary school experience. I had little interest in any sport when I entered the Prep, only to find that the place was obsessed with basketball, a game I had never played and knew nothing about. Intramural basketball competition began shortly after the school year opened. Each homeroom fielded a team and they fought it out on the macadam court between the school and LaSalle Hall. Some of my classmates came to the Prep with expectations of glory playing for the Cavalier varsity. Most of us understood that a pickup game on the macadam court was likely to be the extent of our participation.

Prep, despite its small size, was a powerhouse in the Catholic League. In fairness, few of the other schools were very large either. But the Prep players were smarter overall than their opponents and had excellent coaching. The coach during my years there was John Gallagher, a bear of a man for whom winning was everything. As with all staff members at the Prep, Gallagher had to teach a full load of classes in addition to coaching. He taught health, a state requirement that he knew was a joke and that we knew he knew was a joke. The classes were entertaining unless he perceived that he was being challenged. He was capable of cruel, biting sarcasm if he thought a student deserved it. In that he was no different from some of the other teachers, but he was much better at it. He was not a man to be crossed.

As a basketball coach, Gallagher was preeminently successful. And we loved him for it. We proudly wore our purple-and-gold Eisenhower-style jackets with the words Scranton Prep emblazoned on the back. We were a presence everywhere in the Lackawanna and Wyoming Valleys. We were a basketball powerhouse and we knew it. No wonder students at other schools resented us. In some ways, I admit, we were insufferable.

From knowing nothing and caring less about basketball, I was transformed into an avid fan. Varsity members were my heroes. They were everyone's center of attention, a center I longed to get close to. I had my chance at the beginning of my second year when a position as basketball manager became available. There were three managers, one from each of the three upper classes. That made me the junior manager for the 1953-54 season. As described earlier, part of my duties was to schlep basketballs to and from daily practices at the Pennsylvania Oral School in Green Ridge or the South Scranton Junior High School.

That meant I attended those practices and learned the wisdom of basketball from Gallagher, who was an excellent teacher. His philosophy was simple: play smart and play defense. He had played in a professional league at one time and was able to show his players physically how to perform the maneuvers he advocated. He did not tolerate mediocrity and was never willing to accept defeat. He was legendary in the Catholic League for his courtside histrionics and his periodic challenges of the referees.

One referee, Nunzi Semenza, was a personal friend of Gallagher's and occasionally showed up at practice. Semenza was assigned from time to time to referee games between the Prep and other schools, but no one seemed to think his friendship with Gallagher was a problem. In today's world someone would inevitably blow the whistle. Athletics were important then, particularly to Gallagher, but everyone knew they were just a game.

I learned a great deal from the coach and as time went on he recognized that I knew a lot about the game even though I had absolutely no talent for playing it. He asked me to scout some of our upcoming opponents. Scouting was something Gallagher believed in. When his teams took to the floor, they knew exactly who they were playing and exactly what to expect. That really mattered in close games. I was proud to be asked to serve as a scout, even though the opponents I evaluated were not thought to be a real threat. Gallagher seemed pleased with my reports and I know he included nuggets from those reports in his pre-game instructions. I enjoyed being in the locker room with the players both at practice and particularly during the games. I liked being near the action even if I could not participate directly.

Gallagher was a great motivator and I believe that experience had a great effect on the trajectory of my life. He was an unrelenting taskmaster. Expecting that one should always do his best; anything less was totally unacceptable. That is a difficult model to follow in life, but it leads more often to success than to failure.

In my final year at the Prep, I was the senior basketball manager, which meant I served as scorekeeper for the team. The scorekeeper for the home team was always official scorekeeper for the game. The visiting team's scorekeeper sat with him at the scorer's table. Their mutual task was to keep each other honest. The scorekeeper not only kept track of the score but also the timeouts and other statistics of importance. At the end of the game, the official scorekeeper phoned in the results to the newspaper, which wanted a brief recap of the game as well. The newspapers often assigned reporters for major games, but they still wanted the statistics and the scorekeeper was their source.

At major tournaments, an independent scorekeeper was assigned. He was flanked by the scorekeepers for the opposing teams, assigned to keep all three of them honest. I recall one tournament game at the Catholic Youth Center. It was the annual Lynett tournament, named for the family that owned the major newspaper in town and was a major benefactor of the Diocese of Scranton, owner and operator of the CYC. The Lynett tournament was a big deal and Prep was almost always invited. I can't recall the opponent in the finals that year, but it was a very close game. During the second half, I noticed that the official scorer had neglected to record a timeout taken by Prep. When several minutes went by and he failed to correct the error, I surreptitiously erased the record of the timeout from my scorebook. The next time Gallagher called a timeout, he queried me as to how many were left. I signaled him the number reflected in my record and that of the official scorer. He looked at me quizzically and I nodded affirmatively. He understood.

Later in the game, when Gallagher called his final timeout the coach and scorer for the opposing team protested vigorously. The officials came to the scorer's table and examined the official scorebook as well as my book and that of our opponents. They had no alternative but to declare the final Gallagher timeout as valid. We won the game. Gallagher never mentioned the incident to me, but I'm sure he knew what had gone on. At that point in my life I had yet to learn that the end does not justify the means. On the other hand, I understood intuitively that what I had done was nothing to be proud of, so I kept it to myself.

Basketball took up much of the school year, beginning with intramurals shortly after classes resumed and culminating in post-season competition leading to the state championship. It was also the major social catalyst during the year. Packs of Marywood girls joined their male counterparts at all home games. After the games, virtually everyone streamed north on Cedar Avenue to Tony Harding's all-night diner. Tony Harding's and Yank's Diner downtown near the Cathedral were two major late-night hangouts from my years at the Prep through graduation from the university. After the basketball games, the packs of males gathered at one group of tables and the packs of females at others nearby. There was plenty of friendly conversation between the tables but little pairing off. Most of that had occurred after the games when couples headed off on their own to pursue their relationships outside the prying eyes of the packs.

After a season of basketball, we were exhausted and looking forward to the summer vacation. Yet there was a brief spring baseball season and Prep always fielded a competitive team. Gallagher coached baseball as well as basketball. There was nothing that man could not do. In my junior year I decided to try out for the baseball team. I should have known better. After I nearly was hit in the head by a fly ball, Gallagher banished me from the field—for my own safety, he explained. That did not temper the disappointment, frustration and shame I felt as I made my way home. In my mind he had humiliated me, but I still loved him. At home, I sobbed uncontrollably as I sought to come to grips with my shame.

Never one to step back from a challenge I decided to try out the following year as a catcher. Who would be crazy enough to want to stoop behind home plate as a baseball came hurtling toward you and as a batter tried to hit it? There was only a split second from the moment when the ball was in position for the batter to hit it and it came crashing into the catcher's mitt. If the catcher flinched, the ball could career off the glove into his face mask and out of play. While I was willing to work behind the plate I didn't have the talent for that either. A good catcher has to be aware of everything going on along the base paths. When a runner tries to steal second base, the catcher has to be prepared to throw him out. I had a hard enough time just catching the majority of pitches to be concerned with the base paths. Predictably, I did not make the cut, but at least I had not been humiliated.

Other than basketball and baseball, we did not have any interscholastic athletics at the Prep. A few of our classmates played golf. I can't remember anyone who played tennis, which most of us considered effete. Even though we didn't play golf, several of us caddied two summers at the Elmhurst County Club. We did not consider golf a sport, but it was a welcome source of income. Caddies were independent contractors, not employees. If you caddied you got paid; if you didn't, you went home with nothing. Thus, it was advisable to get to the country club early to add you name to the list of caddies available for that day. Since we were too young to drive, we had to rely on hitch-hiking. If we were lucky a club member would notice us thumbing a ride on Moosic Street and transport us all the way to the club.

Caddies were assigned in the order of sign-up. This was in the period before universal availability of powered golf carts so most golfers signed up for caddies. Each of us carried two bags. The procedure called for us to walk partly down the fairway to determine where our golfers' drives had landed. Theoretically, that was not a problem, but many of the golfers we caddied for at Elmhurst had a propensity to hit their balls into the woods that lined the fairways. Their ineptitude was matched only by their anger when we were unable to pinpoint exactly where the errant missiles had landed. Carrying two golf bags for 18 holes in the heat of summer was difficult enough. When it was coupled with inconsiderate golfers the experience was downright unpleasant.

Interestingly, I did not become interested personally in golf until my mid 50s, and it never occurred to me why I had not taken up the game much earlier. When Edward reminded me of the unpleasant experiences we both endured as caddies at the Elmhurst County Club I understood.

21

The Funnel

Thirty of the 37 young men who graduated in 1956 from Scranton Prep matriculated at the University of Scranton. Two went to Notre Dame. Joe Dorsey was recruited to play basketball for Holy Cross, a small Jesuit liberal arts college in Worcester, MA, that had contributed Bob Cousy and Tom Heinsohn to the NBA. Two went to King's College in Wilkes-Barre, one to Villanova and one to Catholic University in Washington, D.C. All went to Catholic institutions of higher education. Most of us went to the university because it was inexpensive, it was Jesuit and we could live at home. I have absolutely no regrets about that decision. The same cannot be said for some other Prep graduates, who feel that we were funneled into the university to meet the needs of the Jesuits rather than our own. They contend that many of us could have gone on to "name" institutions well within our intellectual capabilities.

That may be true, for I found myself to be the intellectual equal of all students, including graduates of the most famous "name" schools, when I pursued postgraduate education in two unrelated professions. But was it a disservice to funnel us into the university? At that time there seems to have been some disagreement even among the Jesuits. The university dean, Father William G. Kelly, SJ, told a small group of us seeking a change from one class to another that Prep graduates "think they run the place." It was clear that he was sure he ran the place and resented any implication that he shared that responsibility with anyone, much less a group of lowly students. I wonder if he knew that he was known on campus as Jelly Belly Kelly.

In a sense Father Kelly was right. Prep graduates were prominently involved in virtually all campus activities. Perhaps that was related to one valid observation made by those critical of the funnel phenomenon. It was clear from the start that we were much better prepared for college work than our classmates, most of whom came from small parochial high schools up and down the line. There was a small contingent of boarding students and a few from Central High School. Both groups, by and large were as well prepared as we were. Since we found the work in the first year unchallenging, we were lured into heavy participation in extracurricular activities. My profile in the 1960 Windhover, our yearbook, lists participation in 10 separate activities, in many of which I served as an officer. That schedule most assuredly got in the way of academic achievement.

For me, it was a blessing. I had enrolled in the Physics program. Physics was the only science with which I had any familiarity. Remember, I took Greek at the Prep. We all took physics in our senior year there and I was fascinated that there was a scientific explanation—and mathematical calculation—for even the most commonly observable phenomena. I left the program after two years, not because I could not do the work but because it no longer interested me. This apparently was a manifestation of the recurrent boredom phenomenon that worried Mother. I knew I could do the work because I had done well in the first heavy duty science class in freshman year. We started with basic chemistry. It was a big class, since all science students—physics chemistry, biology and pre-engineering—were required to take it. On the first day of class, Professor Paul Waters asked if there were any students in the class who had had no exposure to chemistry. I was among four who raised their hands. Two of us were among the four students who earned As for our work in the first semester.

I was not turned off by the science, but was frustrated with the math instruction in the first year. Math had always come easily to me so this was unexpected. I and several other Prep graduates enrolled in the science curriculum signed up for a class to be taught by a professor with an excellent reputation. How surprised we were when a substitute showed on the first day of class and announced the scheduled professor had taken a sabbatical and the substitute would be our instructor for the semester. That would not have been a problem if he had been competent, but he wasn't. This led directly to our confrontation with Jelly Belly Kelly, vice president and dean of studies. Frustrated at the incompetence of our instructor, four of us asked to be transferred to a night school class being taught by someone known to be competent. Kelly did not understand that we were his customers. He was intransigent, as well as arrogant and unpleasant. I doubt his approach would be tolerated at the university—or any other institution—today.

I did not recognize it at the time, but that was the beginning of the end. I was fortunate that I managed to complete two years of the physics curriculum, since that provided me with the bulk of the prerequisites for medical school, a career I was not contemplating at the time. When I decided to change majors, I selected English, following the lead of Bill Connolly and others who left the sciences for the arts. I guess that meant I had no idea of what I wanted to do but I knew that I no longer wanted to be a scientist.

One thing I should have known is that whatever I chose to do in life, I wanted to be in charge. Shortly after classes began at the university a group of Prep graduates got together to discuss the election of class officers. It was decided that Gene Kelley, who had been our class president at the Prep would be our candidate for that office at the university. Frank McDonnell was to be the campaign manager and we were all to work in the campaign. Shortly after that I met a cousin who also had ambitions to be president of the freshman class. He was Cy (for Cyril) O'Hara. Cy had recently left the Marine Corps with the rank of captain. He was a very impressive guy—and he was a cousin, a son of Alberta Maguire O'Hara, who in turn was a daughter of Michael Maguire, the twin of my grandfather. It is fascinating that the twin brothers, Michael Maguire and Edward McGuire spelled their names differently. I have copies of both death certificates, which confirm the variance.

We were still boys but Cy was a man. I decided to be his campaign manager. I could not resist the opportunity to be in charge of a campaign instead of working for Frank McDonnell on behalf of my friend, Gene Kelley. I went to Kelley and explained. He said he understood, but our friendship was never the same. How could I expect him to understand when I did not fully understand my compulsion to be in charge until many years later?

Cy and I waged a vigorous campaign but we lost. Frank McDonnell was much more skilled at politics than I. He has gone on to be a successful lawyer in Scranton and recently completed a term as chairman of the university's board of trustees. I never expected any less of him.

Failure as a politician did not diminish my interest in the subject. I became active in the political science club, which taught parliamentary procedure to high school students in preparation of a model senate conducted by the club each year for those students. It was also was the university organization that sent a delegation annually to the Intercollegiate Conference on Government in Harrisburg. To teach parliamentary law one had to learn it. That effort eventually paid off at the 1960 ICG, as described earlier.

The University Players also engaged my efforts for part of the year. I was part of the cast for the university's production of *Twelve Angry Men* as well as some other productions lost to memory. One production I recall in particular was *Teahouse of the August Moon*. I served as prop manager for the production, which meant I had to scour the town for the various effects that would be used on stage. The biggest challenge was getting a military Jeep. I headed to the Watrous Armory and made my case to the local National Guard leadership. Scranton was headquarters of the 109th Infantry, part of Pennsylvania's 28th Infantry, known as the "bloody bucket division" based on the red keystone patch on their uniforms.

The 109th had plenty of Jeeps. I was sure they could spare one. I had yet to become familiar with what was known at the time as government "red tape." The 109th had plenty of Jeeps and said it would be happy to spare one. But none of us was in the military and, therefore, they could not allow us to drive one of their vehicles the few blocks from the armory to the Masonic Temple, where the production was scheduled. Well, then, what would be acceptable? I expected them to volunteer someone to drive it for us, but that thought apparently did not cross their minds. Eventually, we agreed to rent a truck to carry the Jeep to the Masonic Temple and back. It took a lot of manpower to load and unload the prop, but it was in place on opening night. If nothing else, I was a problem solver.

Another exciting activity was the campus newspaper, The Aquinas. The editor my freshman year was the flamboyant Bill Kiesling, whose position at The Tribune I was asked to fill the summer after graduation. Kiesling was always stirring the pot. He originated the homeliest man on campus (HMOC) contest and arranged for the winner to have an all-expense-paid date with a campus queen, selected by a process I've forgotten. Since we had no women at the university, the campus queen invariably came from Marywood College. The homeliest man was selected by vote of the student body based on photos published in The Aquinas. I had limited exposure to the newspaper under Kiesling but I decided as a sophomore to devote more time to it. John Rafferty had succeeded Kiesling as editor. Rafferty was a serious student in the classics curriculum and very well informed of world events. He had been a master debater while at the Prep. The managing editor was Bill Connolly, who had artistic as well as editorial talent. He produced many editorial cartoons, including a depiction of the ideal candidate for homeliest man on campus.

Rafferty and Connolly taught me the rudiments of journalism as they knew it. Rafferty worked as a neighborhood correspondent for The Tribune and was somewhat knowledgeable in the newspaper style of writing. I can remember being dumfounded that news articles were written from scratch on a typewriter rather than being written out longhand and then typed. I learned to hunt and peck my way through a story and to make editorial changes with a pencil so that the typesetter could understand what I intended to say. I learned to read proof and to write headlines. What really interested me was designing the newspaper, laying out exactly where the stories would go and how they would look. The paper was published every other week during the school year and editorial preparation the night it was "put to bed"—meaning the night before it went to the printer—usually lasted until after midnight. Whenever it ended, we usually headed off to O'Toole's for a nightcap.

After a year of preparation, I felt I was ready for the top job. That compulsion to be in charge propelled my ambition, which was encouraged by Connolly. Rafferty and I had a "come to Jesus" meeting and he agreed to hand over the editorship. To his everlasting credit, in my mind, he continued to work with me and was very supportive during my term. I came to regard him as my closest friend at the university. He went on to a career in the military and later as an information technology executive before retiring to Western Virginia a few years ago.

Being in charge did not, in and of itself, confer good judgment. Father William N. Tome, SJ, the faculty advisor to The Aquinas, had better things to do than censor the campus newspaper. He had little criticism of most issues, but there were limits to what would be tolerated. One breach of judgment came after a group of Marywood College students demonstrated at the university for or against some cause. The issue is lost forever, but the fallout remains vivid in my memory. We covered the demonstration with photos and an unflattering description of the demonstrators. As I recall they were described in one reference as "bellowing buffaloes." Father Tome took a lot of heat on that one and everyone knows what flows downhill. That breach of judgment didn't help my sister, Ellen, who was a freshman at Marywood College at the time. Many of her classmates considered her tainted by her sibling relationship with me.

And then there was my confrontation with Pete Carlesimo, the athletic director. Pete was one of those Scranton fixtures who seemed to enjoy a lifetime appointment. He had played football at Fordham in the late 1930s and came to the university as head football coach in 1944. At one time or another, Pete coached football, basketball and cross-country at the university. He was not a man to be trifled with, particularly by a mere student during an interview about the athletic program. I have absolutely no recollection of the issue but I recall quite well that I was concerned during the interview that Pete would come from behind his desk and do me serious bodily harm. I heard from Father Tome after that one as well. At the time I did not mind being called to account. I recognized that the university was my publisher and, as A.J. Liebling wrote: "Freedom of the press is important if you own the press."

I did not recognize then that I would never own the press and that would be a significant issue in the journalism career I expected to follow. Both Connolly and I expected to be journalists. During my junior year, he told me about the Columbia University Graduate School of Journalism in New York. One weekend, he and I boarded a bus for New York. We walked up Broadway from the Port Authority terminal—a facility with which I would become quite familiar during my year in New York—to the Columbia campus on Morningside Heights. The subway would have been much more efficient, but we were unfamiliar with New York at the time. The J School was at the corner of Broadway and 116th Street, right inside one of the main gates to the campus. We walked around the journalism building and invaded the lobby, but it was a Saturday and no one was available to give us a tour. While we were disappointed, that trip installed the concept of Columbia as a postgraduate option in my mind.

In the second semester of my senior year when I was forced to come to grips with what I would do with the rest of my life, I chose to apply there and, wonder of wonders, was accepted. It did not hurt that a J-School graduate, Ned Gerrity, a former city hall reporter for The Scranton Times who went on to be a top executive at International Telephone and Telegraph, wrote a letter of recommendation on my behalf. I sent him a note of thanks and he responded, asking me to call him several months later "so we can have lunch." Ned was a busy man; we never had lunch.

During my year in New York, Connolly was assigned to Armed Forces Radio, near Columbus Circle in Manhattan. We met often in the evening after work for dinner, a few drinks and discussions reminiscent of those we had had for years while at the university. I believe at the time that he wanted to pursue a career in broadcast journalism. His distinguished career was in newspaper journalism, primarily at The New York Times, so neither us appears to have followed the path we expected. One thing Connolly expected to do was complete the journalism program at Columbia and he did, entering two years after me when he had satisfied his military obligation.

Since that time, my life has had many twists and turns, some voluntary and some a result of events outside of my control. And while there are many interesting stories I could tell about those experiences, they are outside the scope of this memoir. One thing I can say with conviction, I bear no resentment or disappointment that I was among those funneled into the university. Those four years provided me countless useful experiences, the memories of which are fondly recalled.

22

Epilogue: Alpha and Omega

The reader may recall that this memoir grew out of a request made by my niece, Ellen Mrha, to share memories I had of her mother, the 15th anniversary of whose untimely death was approaching. The initial e-mail installment of the 25-message series follows:

April 3, 2005

Ellen,

The first remembrance is a no-brainer. I mentioned to Coralie that she might have to assist me with the memories. She immediately cited the incident that I already had decided to be the first installment.

You may recall that when your Mother was living with us in Lincolnshire she had a close friend named Linda Burton, who worked with me at the hospital. Coralie and I were traveling somewhere and your Mother and Linda were looking after the house.

At the time I had about 40 cases of wine stored in the cellar against a cool wall. There was wine of every variety and quality. Among the most prized bottles were 10 cases of 1982 Bordeaux I had purchased as futures that were considered "too young" to drink at that time. Possibly the prized of the prized was a case of Chateau Latour—a "first growth," one or two bottles of which are still in my cellar.

When Coralie and I returned, either Ellen or Linda remarked casually that they really appreciated my fine wines. Come to find out that of all the hundreds of bottles they had randomly chosen the Latour to sample. They reported that it was good—so good that they had another bottle.

I'm glad they enjoyed it.

Love,

Uncle Terry

Obviously, the event recounted in that message occurred many years after I had come of age in Scranton and headed off to New York and beyond. I and both of my siblings had had many experiences in the intervening years. There is no reasonable way to assemble and report those experiences. The best I can do is to paint a reasonable picture of what life was like in our childhood and early adulthood. Necessarily, that picture is reported as seen through my eyes. Presumably my life and the lives of my siblings were profoundly affected by the milieu in which we were reared and came of age. For anyone interested in who any of us is or was, I hope this work will prove useful.

Necessarily, the focus of these stories is who we were and what our early life was like. Neglected was the issue of where and who we came from. That topic was the subject of my final e-mail to Ellen, which follows:

April 28, 2005

When I reflect back on our childhood, I can't help but think that if Mother and Father were still alive, they would be the great-grandparents of Ann Marie, Coralie, Stavros, Trinity and Leah, the children of Terry, Andrea and Jean Marie. That reminds me that I and my siblings were the great-grandchildren of Terence and Mary Gerrity Carden, Michael and Bridget Martin Walsh, Michael and Margaret Gilmartin Brogan and Thomas and Bridget Tighe McGuire.

We don't know a lot about these folks. We're not even sure that Bridget Martin's husband was named Michael, but the odds are good. They were all immigrants from Ireland. We're not sure from where exactly, but family lore puts their origin in County Mayo on the west coast where Ireland meets the Atlantic. It is well known in County Mayo that a great many folks from the town of Ballina and its surrounding area immigrated to Scranton. There is also reason to suspect that most of our forebears came from the area near Killala, west of Ballina. It's not hard to understand why it was common for immigrants from a certain area to congregate in the New World. The only thing missing here is documentation. The trail of our forebears ends at the water's edge. We have been unable to identify them from any of the passenger manifests or other records that might tell us when and how they came here.

Then as now, County Mayo was part of the Gaeltacht, the Irish-speaking portion of the country. Folks there were poor and were devastated by the potato famine. Many of them were among the million who left that sad island and, fortunately for us, were not among the million who died of starvation and disease while grain and cattle continued to be exported to Mother England. This was a sad chapter in the history of humanity, but it was to cause a tide of immigration to America of folks who made and whose progeny continue to make a huge impact on their new home.

I spell my paternal great-grandfather's name with one r because that is what is on his gravestone. I remember that Father was very particular about the spelling of his name, but I'm not sure he ever saw his grandfather's gravestone. It was in a remote section of the Cathedral Cemetery in Scranton. Uncle Bob took me there one day and told me a remarkable story about Terence, a story that may be entirely or most certainly partially mythical.

It was Uncle Bob's hypothesis that Terence Carden was a firebrand, a rebel, a member of the dreaded Molly Maguires, which terrorized mine owners and foremen in the anthracite mining areas of Pennsylvania in the 19th century. Desperate men do desperate things, and the men could do little else to protest the inhumane conditions in the pits. Nevertheless, it is highly unlikely Great-grandfather was affiliated with the Molly Maguires, who were centered in the southern minefields in and around Pottstown and Hazleton. There is no evidence that they had penetrated Lackawanna County, which actually did not even exist at the time. Scranton was then part of Luzerne County. Also a search of what records there are of Molly Maguire membership failed to identify anyone named Terence Carden or any alternative forms of that name.

It is not hard to believe that Terence could have been a firebrand and that it could have gotten him in trouble. From observations of myself, Edward, Father and Uncle Bob, I do not find it unlikely that my great-grandfather was a man willing—even anxious—to express his opinion, particularly when and if he encountered what he considered injustice. Tolerance was not endemic in Scranton at the time. The Irish were expected to work hard and keep their mouths shut.

Uncle Bob believed that Terence was on the lam from the authorities when he died. He told me that Terence had escaped from jail and had injured himself when he was forced to jump over a fence to evade the police. His wound got infected and in the absence of effective treatment died. His burial in an obscure section of the cemetery was interpreted by Uncle Bob as evidence that Terence's friends and cohorts were out to hide the body from the authorities. The anonymity of the gravesite was confirmed when a genealogist I commissioned to help trace our family tree found no evidence of it in the records of the Cathedral Cemetery. I have no doubt it is there, since I saw it and I remember in particular that Terence was spelled with one r.

Uncle Bob seems to have been right about one thing. Terence apparently died of infection, "orchitis," according to his death certificate. That is an unusual diagnosis as a cause of death. Orchitis technically means inflammation of a testicle or testicles. It does not commonly lead to death. However, there is a very serious infection of the scrotum that leads to gangrene and death. It is Fournier's disease, which is a bacterial infection of the scrotum, leading to severe swelling that a doctor in the late 19th century could have described as "orchitis." And, it could have developed from a wound suffered in leaping over a fence.

There were no antibiotics in those days and there would have been nothing they could have done for him except offer the comfort of morphine or, more likely, tincture of opium. I have seen only one case of Fournier's disease in my career and will never forget it. The patient was a middle-aged black man who was admitted from the emergency room of Philadelphia General Hospital while I was a medical student. I encountered him on the ward and knew immediately that this was a serious matter. He was transferred to the intensive care unit where he died just as I was plunging a needle into his back to extract fluid that had accumulated in his chest cavity. It was an experience I will never forget. When I saw the diagnosis on my great-grandfather's death certificate, that memory flooded back into my consciousness.

There are no comparable tales or myths attached to any of our other great-grandparents, but I am sure interesting tales could be told if only we knew them. I suppose this has been part of my motivation for preparing these installments. I am sure that they are not what I expected when I began and doubt they are what you, Ellen, anticipated when you asked me to send remembrances of your Mother.

But I do think they shed some light on the childhood of the three Carden siblings in Scranton in the 1940s and 1950s. They also touch on those who came before us, where they came from and to some extent what kind of people they were. We now have a lineage that stretches back six generations, where we lose its origins at the water's edge. That's OK, since we have more than enough material to work with right here.

Siochan agus beannacht
Peace and blessings,

Uncle Terry

Terence Carden continues to be a mysterious figure in my consciousness. Perhaps I became intrigued initially by the myth of his involvement with the Molly Maguires and perhaps because of the spelling variant on his headstone. Perhaps I make too much of the variant, based presumably on my early training in getting everyone's name exactly right in an obituary. We've already seen that twin brothers Edward McGuire and Michael Maguire seemingly found nothing unusual in the variant spellings of their names. So, who knows if Terence knew or cared about how his name was spelled. He may very well have been illiterate. In the 1880 census document I recently obtained through a friend in Ohio, he was listed as Terrence. His death certificate could be read either way, but most probably has two Rs. Maybe I placed too much trust in the care shown by the person who carved the headstone.

978-0-595-36329-2
0-595-36329-6

Printed in the United States
50701LVS00005B/45